FROM INDIANA to Utah's CANYON COUNTRY

MISADVENTURES FROM THE LIFE OF FRED RADCLIFFE

by

Fred Radcliffe

Fred, 1930

EDITED BY T. L. LEWIS

Published by
Canyon Country Publications
of Moab, Utah
for
Fred Radcliffe

This book was published in
the interest of preserving in print
some of the colorful human history
of the Canyon Country region and the
stories of the equally colorful people
who have been drawn by its
unique natural history.

Fred, 1943

All pictures credited to F. A. Barnes
are used with his permission
and are copyrighted
by the photographer

Artwork by
Rick Showalter

Published 1993 by
Canyon Country Publications

CONTENTS

CHAPTER ONE

THE EARLY YEARS

I was born in Indianapolis, Indiana on March 20, 1921, destined to remain an only child. There were advantages and disadvantages to this condition, but I was stuck with it and, in the long run, it worked out well. We lived in a rural area a few miles west of the Indianapolis city limits. Growing up in a non-urban community offered a number of opportunities that city children missed out on. My earliest recollection of life at 535 South Cole Street was the existence of an invisible line outside the house that I knew I was not to cross. There was no fence, only a very small bush but, oh, how I longed to venture beyond that tiny bush.

My first piece of rolling stock was an old goat wagon. I don't remember using that wagon much, but I know it was my first love in what was to be a lifelong succession of passionate affairs with both two- and four-wheeled vehicles. In today's modern, efficient world, every vehicle, regardless of its make and model, is tediously similar in appearance to its competitor. But in those early times, an automobile had its own special styling that distinguished it from any other. Those were the days of the great, sleek monsters, each with its own personality. In the 1920s and the early '30s, I developed a talent for quickly identifying from afar just about any type of approaching vehicle. I'd stand between my Uncle Arch's knees and call out the names of cars that most younger people today have never heard of: Pierce-Arrow, Cole, Graham-Paige, Locomobile, Stutz, Marmon, Oakland, Whippet, Star, Nash, Stearns-Knight, Durant, Erskine, Oakland, Chandler and even the Apperson Jackrabbit, just to name a few.

In the early twenties, my dad worked for Messenger's, a large furniture company in downtown Indianapolis. He was later offered a better position with Bob Iselin's Rug Company, where he stayed until 1926. Although Bob and Dad were good friends, my father felt a pressing need to establish his own business. He quit Iselin's and he and my mother took a giant step forward, opening a small used furniture store on Howard Street in West Indianapolis. They rented a building 24 feet wide and sixty feet long. Mother made a drape which we hung in the rear of the store, affording us a separate living space. Apparently, Dad made an ample sum of money selling that old used stuff, because soon he was able to transfer his inventory into a larger building. We no longer had to live in the store, but moved into what we then considered to be the lap of luxury, a two-story house of our own.

Everything was going along fine until I started running around with some worldly big-city boys and we got caught stealing from a cracker barrel at the local market. I still vividly remember that night, when my dad took me past the county jail and pointed it out to me, saying, *"Young man, that's where you'll end up if you keep hanging around with that bunch, stealing crackers!"* The message came through loud and clear and that put an end to my budding criminal career. Come to think of it, about that same time Dad suddenly decided I'd be better off back at our home outside the city. My folks seemed more content, too, after returning to that serene rural setting.

I entered the second grade in School Number Fourteen, and kept virtually all of the same classmates clear through high school. One of my favorite buddies was Emory Turner, who, after graduation, became one of my motorcycling companions and remains a close friend to this day. It was interesting to observe the camaraderie which developed among classmates in our school days. We were almost like a big family. Oddly enough, none of the individuals in our closely-knit group ever grew up to marry a fellow classmate. As I mentioned, the same group stuck together through high school and I've often wondered if this closeness among us was unusual. Perhaps it was attributable to living through the Depression days together.

I think I was approaching the ripe old age of ten years when I first tried my hand at marbles. Now, in order to appreciate the finer points of marble-playing, one must become familiar with the different types of marbles and their respective purposes. The ones used as "shooters" were agate marbles. These had to be a bit larger than the "immies" or imitation agates made from glass, also sometimes called "glassies." I can't recall how much a good "aggie" cost, but it must have been a veritable fortune - at least 25 cents. Only a well-heeled kid could afford the luxury of owning a quality agate. The use of "steelies" was generally discouraged, as they tended to break the glassies. However, there were some veteran players whose glassies had survived vicious attacks by steelies and bore the battle scars to prove it - milky, moon-shaped flaws in their centers. There was always one expert shooter in the neighborhood and Ed Stegemoller was the man to beat. His hands seemed to be twice the size of other boys'. He rarely lost a game, and when he did it was the talk of the neighborhood for weeks.

My cohorts and I were also avid kite pilots. We flew two types of kites, a two-sticker and a three-sticker. The two-stick kite was designed for flying in light winds. A three-sticker flew higher and held up better in the stronger gusts. Those three-stickers were great for "kite fights" but they required some pretty hefty string. I remember trying on several occasions to keep a kite up in the air all night. I never made it, though, because the winds and I both died down simultaneously a few hours after sundown. The cost involved in building either type of kite was probably less than twenty cents. When a kite shredded, we'd rebuild it using grocery sack paper, which actually lasted much longer than the original kite paper.

Trips to the grocery store provided me with some entertaining diversion. My mother would write out a list of items she needed and I'd run it to the store and give it to the grocer. He'd hurry about the store, filling the order. Some foods like crackers, pickles and peanut butter were in big wooden barrels and he'd scoop them out in the quantities Mom specified. On the way home, I would invariably pick up two or three friends and we'd end up making a detour through this old, empty three-room house down the block. We'd play around inside and eventually work our way up onto the roof, then we'd jump from the roof of the house to the roof of the garage,

7

then to the ground. Then we'd run back through the house, up onto the roof again, and so on. By that time, I'd generally have forgotten all about the groceries. After a few good jumps, some neighbor would spot us and end up calling the law. We learned to expect this and always kept an eye out for the Sheriff's car. We could see him approaching two blocks away and were always long gone by the time he arrived. Despite all my good intentions, I frequently came home missing some of the items on the grocery list. Even so, my mother still thought I was a good boy, perhaps just a little forgetful. I hope she never had any idea how close three or four "good boys" came to destroying an empty three-room house and garage.

Dad's mother died when he was nine years old; as a result, his schooling was very limited. I once asked Dad how far he went in school and he confessed that he'd received only two years of formal education. Despite that handicap, his skills in mathematics and other subjects seemed to be on a level with many people who had completed high school, and his vocabulary certainly belied his brief time in the schoolroom.

In 1929, on a tip from a banker friend that the stock market was looking shaky, Dad pulled out 900 dollars which he had in a building-and-loan outfit and purchased a 120-acre farm in Morgan County, just one mile from Eminence, Indiana. During the early Depression days, he picked up some adjacent parcels here and there and ultimately ended up with about 280 acres of rich farmland. To his credit, he acknowledged my distaste for farming. In fact, when a friend asked, *"Roy, what's Fred goin' to do with that farm when you die?"* my dad replied, *"He'll probably trade it for a motorcycle and a gallon of gas and head out west someplace!"* Well, I showed him. I sold that darn farm years later for a lot more than my Dad paid for it. I also got some satisfaction from the fact that he subsequently caught the motorcycle fever, too, and had to eat his words. He was always a bit of a speed demon, although driving fast back in the 1920s was quite a bit different from driving fast in more recent years. There was an expression in the late '20s, "going like sixty," which, back then, was as nearly inconceivable as reaching the speed of sound!

Now, ask any Hoosier and he'll tell you with absolute certainty that Indiana was the birthplace of the sport of basketball. I can't recall the exact year I got my first basketball, but it was when I was about twelve years old, so that would be around 1933. The Stegemoller family next door had four

8

boys, each a year apart in age. Bill Stegemoller and I were the same age. Edwin, the marble ace, was one year younger and he and Kenny Hampton, who lived down the block, rounded the team out to four players. Dad helped us put up the basket on the garage, but about a year later somebody in our gang scrounged up an old telephone pole and we set up a court out on my father's extra lot. This gave us more room and also eliminated our having to interrupt the game to go behind the garage and retrieve the ball when we overshot not only the basket, but the whole building. I tried out for the elementary school team, thinking that my neighborhood practice would benefit me, but to no avail.

Our mentor and idol in those days was All-American Johnny Wooden of Purdue University. Johnny was from Centerton, a tiny town in Morgan County which probably never boasted a population of more than a hundred people at one time. The nearest high school was in Martinsville. After college, both Johnny and his brother, Maurice "Cat" Wooden, played for the semi-pro Kautsky team in Indianapolis. A competing team, the Zoelnor Pistons in Fort Wayne, Indiana, later became renowned as the Detroit Pistons. "Cat" Wooden went on to become the Ben Davis High School basketball coach. Once again, I tried out for the team, but my 5-foot, 6-inch frame didn't cut the mustard and I ended up on the track team, running the mile and competing in cross country races. Johnny Wooden coached at South Bend Central High School and eventually became a renowned UCLA basketball coach.

My dad really enjoyed the farm and much preferred spending his time there to working in the furniture store, so he hired a store manager, Chuck Harsin, who ran the business while Dad went to the farm on weekends. There were exceptions to this arrangement if Dad's expertise was sorely needed at the store, but Chuck certainly became a valuable asset. As with most rural homes in the early 1930s, we had no electricity at the farm. To provide the family with some evening entertainment, my dad, with Chuck's assistance, rigged up a battery-powered Atwater-Kent radio and ran it off the battery out of the Oldsmobile.

Dad loved horses. It was a hangover from his tobacco-growing days in the bluegrass region of Kentucky. He was also amazingly adept at breaking and training horses. Apparently I didn't inherit my father's affinity for the critters. In fact, I could hardly stand to be near one. The only time I could moderately appreciate a horse was when I used one to pull the hay rake after the hay had been mowed. I was fascinated, however, with the huge threshing rigs that occasionally came down the graveled road outside of

9

Eminence. The operators of the rigs would go from farm to farm, offering their services for pay. I remember the going wage was about one dollar a day and a free lunch. The lunches were really multi-course meals with all the trimmings, worth at least twice what the workers would get paid for that day. It was not unusual for farmers to get together and help each other out whenever needed, sort of a barter system that helped lighten everyone's workload. In retrospect, most ordinary people, my parents included, faced quite a challenge just keeping food on the table. Despite the hardships, though, I don't remember anyone indulging in a moment's self-pity.

It happened that Dad somehow got wind of a little resort called Blue Bluffs, situated on the White River near Martinsville, Indiana. A widow named Mrs. Craig had inherited the place after her husband's demise. She had an attractive home, as well as several cabins which she rented out to visitors. There were three or four very nice guest houses which appealed to some of the more affluent guests, and about twenty rustic cabins which were available on a yearly basis to those of more modest means for a rental fee of fifty dollars apiece. Now, in 1930, with money being so scarce, Dad and Mother gave the matter considerable thought before plunking down fifty bucks for a year's use of one of the log cabins, but plunk they did. It was a good thing, too, because Blue Bluffs and our little cabin, which we dubbed "The Windblew Inn," feature prominently in some of my fondest memories.

Our cabin was a warm and cozy little log structure situated about 75 feet from the bank of the White River and about fifty feet above the river. Huge beech trees surrounded the cabin, but left sufficient room to park two or three automobiles when we had visitors.

There were no power lines from outside to provide electricity to Blue Bluffs, but there was a localized Delco generator system which was capable of providing power to parts of the resort for short periods of time. The generator was shut down at ten o'clock every night except Saturday, when square dances were held in the large dance hall. On these festive occasions, the generator ran well past midnight and Mrs. Craig even went so far as to provide a few low-wattage bulbs to illuminate a small stretch of the dirt road leading into the resort. My father was never much of a square dancer, but my mother dearly loved it. In retrospect, it seems likely that the promise of square dancing one night a week was a motivating factor (at least on my mother's part) in shelling out a substantial chunk of our life savings for the opportunity to stay at the resort.

Although we frequently did without the luxury of the electricity provided by the generator, we still had several kerosene lamps and a deluxe Aladdin-style lamp which gave off a fairly bright light. We cooked on a wood-burning stove and stored our perishable foodstuffs in Mrs. Craig's ice house. Mrs. Craig would make regular trips into Martinsville in her 1924 Ford pickup truck to get supplies and block ice. There was no indoor plumbing in our little cabin, so we hauled water from Mrs. Craig's house or the nearby refreshment stand for drinking and washing. Sometimes a good rain would furnish us with enough fresh water in our rain barrel to last for a few days and we would get a reprieve from the task of hauling it. There was a little privy out back which accommodated our more intimate bathroom needs.

Loath as I was to admit it at the time, I realize now that lugging buckets of water was actually quite a rewarding experience. In addition to affording me an opportunity to explore the area, carrying that heavy water around built up my arm, leg, and back muscles. I may have been a scrawny kid, but I could lift my weight in water, and that's no mean feat! Climbing the 300-foot cliffs right out our back door helped develop my strength and coordination, too. There were several other kids of various ages who stayed at Blue Bluffs and we spent many happy hours scaling those cliffs which were the resort's namesake, and exploring the hundreds of acres that lay beyond them to the west. We covered a lot of territory in our explorations and encountered many a berry bush during our wanderings. Wild, sun-warmed blackberries are absolutely heavenly, but the bushes are also a favorite hiding place for copperheads. Luckily enough, we kids never had a run-in with any poisonous snakes, probably because we were always very respectful of their desire for privacy.

One incident that stands out clearly in my mind is the time when one of my buddies found a child's pedal car which had been discarded by its owner. One of us (I can't rightly remember which one, for some reason) got the crazy idea of dragging that thing up to the top of the cliff and pushing it off, just to see what would happen. This was not nearly as easy as it sounds. There were only two ways to get it up there. One was a long, winding flight of wooden steps which had been built for weekend visitors; the other was a narrow foot trail. We chose the latter. We made it less than halfway up the trail when we could stand it no longer - we simply had to try to make a run down it with somebody driving the pedal car. Naturally, I drew the short straw. I wedged myself into the little car, trying to swallow the lump in my throat as my buddies gave me a push down the steep incline. The car rapidly picked up speed - way too much speed - and I lost all steering control. That car and I flipped over more times than I can count before we finally came to rest at the bottom of the cliff. Needless to say, I was pretty skinned up and found that I had lost much of my enthusiasm for the sport. But it wasn't long before my scrapes healed, and my friends and I dragged that car back to the top of the cliff and, this time, shoved it off by itself. I admit to experiencing a certain satisfaction when I watched that thing beat itself to pieces on its way down!

Dad became acquainted with Doug McDougald, a bachelor who worked as a handyman for Mrs. Craig. It turned out that Doug had built a few boats for river running and my father approached him about building one for us. Doug drew up rough plans for a 14-foot, square-nosed scow. Dad approved the plans and, before summer was over, the boat was launched. I don't know who used it more often, my dad or I, but I know I had lots of fun with it. I would shove off early in the morning and paddle upstream. It would take a good hour to go one mile, and boy, what a workout!

By the middle of October, Dad had already made plans to upgrade the boat. He got a burr under his tail to buy one of those new contraptions called "outboards." After getting stuck with a used Caile outboard engine which turned out to be a real dog, Dad decided it was worth going the extra dollar for a good product and we wound up with a six-horsepower Neptune, made in Muncie, Indiana. Elco, the forerunner of Evinrude, was probably the best on the market, with Johnson a close second, but the Neptune did all right, too.

One night, following a flash flood, my dad, four of his friends, and two of us boys headed upriver to where the White Lick tributary emptied into the White River. Well, I soon found out the underlying reason for Dad's preoccupation with buying an outboard motor. He wanted to seine fish! With the outboard, we could cover a greater distance in a shorter time, thus catching the high water at its peak. During these periods, the fish, in order to escape the muddy river water, would retreat to the quieter waters at the mouth of the tributary. Herding them into the net at these times was generally very successful, albeit illegal! The result this night was a big harvest - and a lot of exciting fun. The neighbors wondered at the sudden popularity of fish fries in our, and our friends', households but we boys were cautioned to keep our adventure a secret.

A fellow from Indianapolis named Tom Prather rented one of the cabins at Blue Bluffs. Tom was a jeweler and watch repairman. His son, Jack, and I became "river chums." Tom had a Johnson outboard, of which Jack made prodigious use. Inevitably, Jack and I began racing each other, which led to the development of new techniques to outdo one another. I found if I shifted my weight to the bow of my boat, I got more speed out of it. I even came up with a method of steering the boat with ropes. One of our favorite diversions was the game of "chicken." We'd race head-on and see how close we could come without colliding. We got so good that our gunwales would pass within six inches of each other. The real fun was when we hit each other's wake and got the ride of our lives!

My grandmother and grandfather came up from Kentucky that summer and I rigged up a top on the boat in anticipation of their visit. This was to shield "Mother Sadie" from the hot sun as I took her on a river tour. Mother Sadie, who was never referred to as Grandma or Grandmother, was about as wide as she was tall. I got her nicely placed mid-ship and headed up the river. We had gone about a mile when I spotted an overhanging willow tree and decided to run under it and scare her like I had done several of my passengers before. Only I had never had the canopy on before. Yep, you got the picture. I wiped the cover right off the boat slicker than a whistle and scared the daylights out of myself. Mother Sadie just sat there in the middle of the boat as though nothing had happened, but I felt like the biggest fool who ever lived!

After having got a little practice under our belts, we young river rats decided that running the river at flood stage was an exhilarating change of pace. My old high school buddy Art Akers, and his brother Paul, came to visit us at the resort and I was determined to show them a good time. I admit I was also anxious to demonstrate my boating prowess. I planned an early start up the White River, with our initial stop being Henderson Bridge, the first place upstream of Blue Bluffs that the river could be crossed. It was a beautiful morning and the weatherman promised sunny and warm weather for the next two days. The current was much swifter than usual with the river nearing flood stage. Since the territory was new to both the boys, I decided to pull in where White Lick empties into the White River so they could look around a bit. We motored a little way up the creek and ate an early lunch. We had only gone a little over a mile since leaving our cabin, and I knew we had to go about five more miles before reaching the Henderson Bridge. The old 6hp engine was running like a dream. In about an hour, we

caught sight of the bridge up ahead. Suddenly, the engine started to race wildly and I thought, *"Oh, no, a sheared pin!"* Shearing a pin is ordinarily no big problem, but with that swiftly moving current it could really mean trouble. I quickly removed the motor and laid it in the bottom of the boat. My plan was to pull the damaged pin out and replace it with a spare I always carried, but the boat started floating rapidly toward a huge tree lodged in the middle of the river. Before we knew it, the boat was swept up against the tree and overturned, dumping the outboard motor, us, and all our gear into the drink! The three of us managed to fight the current back to the boat and push it into the shallow water near the bank. A quick inventory of missing items included, in addition to the motor, one paddle, the food container and the tool box. After emptying the water out of the boat and doing our best to reorganize what was left of our gear, we wasted no time in heading back to Blue Bluffs. The current being as swift as it was, we went downstream without a motor almost as speedily as we had come upstream with one. It occurred to me as we headed home that anyone watching the river near Blue Bluffs might have been caused undue concern if they happened to see our nautical debris floating downstream.

My father was a very understanding man and took the loss of his motor pretty much in stride, but immediately made plans to go up to the Henderson Bridge the next day to try and retrieve it. Several of Dad's friends accompanied us and we succeeded in locating the motor in short order. The river had subsided considerably in the twenty-hour interval since the swamping. My dad really was a fine fellow and, in looking back, I regret not having fully appreciated him. That's probably typical of children, and it's unfortunate that we don't realize how wonderful our parents are until we're grown and have left home. Dad never scolded me for what could have been an expensive mishap; he just commented that it should be chalked up to experience. I hope I can say that I have shown the same consideration to my children and grandchildren.

One of my favorite families at Blue Bluffs was the Parrish clan. There were six boys and one girl, ranging from nine to nineteen years of age. Don, who was my age, and I usually kept that Neptune outboard pretty busy. One day, I approached him about going on an adventure upriver but he had a prior commitment. His younger brother, Bob, asked if he could go in Don's place. I liked Bob a lot, so I told him he was welcome. We packed lunches and planned to be gone until late afternoon.

We put six miles behind us in a little over an hour and found countless intriguing places to explore. We finally reached a perfect sandbar where we spread out our lunch and ate. After lunch, we wandered around and found an excellent two-by-ten-foot plank, which we decided to take back with us, as one never knows when one might need such a thing.

Despite gasoline being less than fifteen cents a gallon, we chose to conserve what we had and float most of the way back downstream. With the water jug and grub on board, we had to put the plank crosswise on the boat and sit on it. Bob sat on the port side and I balanced on the starboard. It couldn't have been a more beautiful day - quiet, with a blue sky and no wind. After about half an hour, I heard Bob snoring. About ten minutes later, I felt my side of the boat scrape across the sandy bottom. Even though I was only twelve years old, I had learned to read the river and I was sure the water on Bob's side of the boat was well over our heads. I quietly shifted my weight and stepped onto the sandbar on my side. This turned that old plank into a teeter-totter and Bob was unceremoniously dumped into the deep water. He came up gasping for air. It took him a minute to get a handle on what had happened, but he was a good sport and seemed to get a kick out of the "plank prank" I'd played on him. The rest of the trip didn't take long, as we used the outboard motor to get home.

Many changes occurred within the next year. I was thirteen years old and an eye exam indicated I was very nearsighted. This came as no surprise to me because for some time I had not been able to see things that others could. I was fitted with eyeglasses, which made me somewhat self-conscious, but was also given a new watch, which made up for it.

My mother had never been too particular about how I looked when I was roaming the cliffs and boating the river, but things changed on Sunday afternoons when we were breaking camp to head back to Indianapolis. There had been a torrential rainstorm this one Saturday evening, resulting in a flood on the White River. A flood always excited me. There is something about a swiftly moving river that attracts a river rat, whether he is ten or sixty years old. My new glasses made that flood much more wondrous, too, as I had never seen things quite so clearly before. Anyway, my mother had me slicked up neat as a pin for our trip home but I just had to go down and watch the river for a few minutes before we left. All the Parrish children were down there, which struck me as odd since all seven kids were rarely in the same place at the same time. Don was holding the end of the old, heavy rope swing we used to play on. *"Hey, Freddie, why don't you take one last*

swing before you go home?" he called. I couldn't resist. I grabbed the rope up high, got way up on the bank and ran as fast as I could. I swung out for what seemed like forever, then back up onto the bank. It was so exhilarating that I just had to do it once more. This time it was even better because I had put my whole heart and soul into it. I went farther and farther and farther and - suddenly, the rope fell limp and I went flying way out into the flooding river. The next thing I knew, I was carried a hundred feet downstream. I could vaguely hear the laughter of the Parrish kids over the roar of the rushing water. I was so surprised that it took a while for me to realize that they had cut the rope! They finally got their long-awaited revenge for the prank I had played on Bob the previous summer. It was pure luck that I had not lost my glasses or ruined my new watch. My mom had a fit as it was when she saw me struggling up the bank with my good Sunday clothes soaked and stained an evil reddish-brown from river mud!

During the summer months, farmers from nearby Centerton and Brooklyn would come to Blue Bluffs on Saturday night to square dance. This was, as I've mentioned, the night my mother most looked forward to. As my dad didn't dance, he sat and chewed the fat with the other men who didn't care for the sport. We kids had a ball playing various games like tag and "slips", a form of hide-and-seek.

All of the farmers were in pretty dire straits during those Depression days, but most of them seemed to be happy anyway. Many of the people who came to the Saturday night square dances arrived in beat-up Model "T" Fords. One of the families always backed theirs right up against a huge beech tree. One night, a bunch of us boys found a cable lying close to the car and got the idea of wrapping one end of it around the beech tree and the other around the rear axle of the car. This we did, leaving a few feet of slack. We then retreated into the darkness to wait. The dance always ended at around midnight, but it seemed like the owners of the Ford would never get through chatting. Finally, the mother rounded up the two children and loaded them into the car. This Model "T" had no starter and the farmer had to crank it to get it going. At last it caught, and the goodbyes were said. The farmer gunned the engine and the car went forward about four feet and came to an abrupt halt, the rear wheels rising several inches off the ground. This, of course, provided tremendous entertainment for those of us hiding in the bushes. Once again, my father never said anything to me about the epi-

18

sode, although I'd lay a dime to a dollar that he knew exactly who was involved! I suspect my dad participated in his share of mischief-making when he was my age; that probably contributed to his infinite patience and understanding with me and my hi-jinx.

I had taken my friend, Bill Stegemoller, down to Blue Bluffs with me that summer. One Saturday night, we were playing tag and Bill spotted me hiding in a boat down on the river. He hollered, *"I see you, Freddie!"* and came running down the bank to jump into the boat and tag me. Just as he jumped, I shoved the boat away from the shore with my paddle. I timed it perfectly - Bill missed the boat and landed right in the river!

In my early teenage years, I got the fever for a bicycle and Dad bought me one. He wasn't really up on bikes and was unaware of the better, more high-tech ones that were becoming available at that time. Instead, he got me an older model with steel and wooden wheels. Apparently, this design was somewhat less than durable and I was somewhat less than gentle, because I broke the rear wheel in short order. As usual, Dad learned from his mistake. He fixed the wheel and found a buyer for the bike who would go a little easier on it than I had. He then bought me one of the new, steel-wheeled bicycles that ended up lasting me the remainder of my bicycling days.

Speedometers for bicycles were just becoming popular, so I saved my lawn-mowing money and bought one which also had an odometer on it and was made by Stewart Warner. I was fourteen years old and was working for Dad at the store. I rode my bike the two miles to school every day. After school, I pedaled six miles to Dad's store, where I performed various odd jobs and earned about two dollars a week. In the evenings, after work, I put the bike in my father's car and rode home with him. After one year of having the speedometer/odometer on my bike, it registered over 3,500 miles!

In late October, my folks winterized the cabin. My friend, Kenny Hampton, and I decided to take one last ride down to Blue Bluffs on our bikes. This was a trip we had made a few times before, and our parents felt comfortable about letting us go by ourselves. We didn't plan to spend more than just a few minutes there before continuing on to Martinsville. Not far from the little village of West Newton, we passed our familiar 10-mile landmark, the vicious dog. Despite the fact that this dog was behind a fence, he always frightened the daylights out of us. We were convinced that his

19

owners had trained him to eat bikers and that one day they would turn him loose on us. Our original plan to ride to Martinsville changed shortly after we crossed the bridge at Blue Bluffs, as time was running short. About two and a half miles out of Blue Bluffs, there was a steep road leading off to the left which climbed up to a "saddle" in the hills, affording us an excellent view of the countryside lying to the west. After reaching the saddle, instead of descending the other side and returning to Indianapolis on State Road 37, we decided to see how fast we could go back down the side of the hill we had just climbed. Wow! That turned out to be a wild ride at about fifty miles an hour down that loose gravel road! At the bottom, where we got back on the Martinsville Road, we met up with a bicycling club from the east side of Indianapolis. Being country kids, we had never seen a multi-speed bicycle with skinny tires before. It's quite possible that they were not even available on the open market in those days. They were certainly different from our standard, balloon-tired bikes and seemed very exotic to us.

CHAPTER TWO

MOTORCYCLES AND MOTORCYCLE RACING

I recall my first experience with actually operating a motorized vehicle. My mother and father had some old friends who had moved to Madison, Indiana. Raymond Jones had a milk route; he picked up raw, fresh milk from the farms and delivered it to a local creamery. I was about fifteen when he asked me if I'd like to ride with him on the milk run. It sounded like more fun than doing chores, so I went. We had made a few stops when Mr. Jones said, *"Frederick,"* (jeez, I hated that name!) *"How would you like to drive this truck?"* I gulped. The truck, by my standards, was huge - all of one-and-a-half tons. *"Why don't you get over here under this wheel and drive a couple of miles?"* I was scared, but was determined to try it anyway. Well, I survived the drive and doubt we even got the truck out of second gear the whole time.

The next summer one of my buddies, Billy Totten, came riding down to Blue Bluffs on a 74-cubic-inch Harley Davidson and took me on my first motorcycle ride. When I got off that monster, I thought, *"Boy, I don't want to ever get on one of those contraptions again!"* Within the year, I'd sing a different tune.

One day, Dad happened to see a strange rig on one of the downtown streets of Madison, Indiana. They called it a motor scooter, but it was actually a 1936 Cushman "Auto-Glide" and it was for sale. Well, Dad took a ride on the Auto-Glide and I rode it, too! Boy, that was quite a thrill. Nothing more was said about the scooter after the ride and I dismissed it from my mind. At least until I got back to Indianapolis and could brag to my friends that I had ridden something akin to a motorcycle!

My father had an aunt who seemed to have difficulty keeping husbands. She was, at that time, being courted by a gentleman named Mr. Dixon. The Depression had hit Mr. Dixon rather hard and he was out of a job. I don't know how he managed it, but Dad finagled Mr. Dixon a job selling motor scooters in Indianapolis. Then one day, Dad came home with one of those Cushman Auto-Glides. This would turn out to be a milestone in both our lives. Dad justified the Auto-Glide purchase by saying that it could be used on his furniture store's collection route. I was just fifteen, so I was only allowed to ride the Auto-Glide on the back roads in the beginning. Kenny Hampton joined me on my first "legal" ride to Blue Bluffs. It was raining lightly. We were doing about forty down a hill near Brooklyn. With no warning whatsoever, the scooter, living up to its name, scooted right out from under us. Kenny went sliding past me, then I went sliding past the scooter, then the scooter passed both of us. Finally, after about a 300-foot slide, Kenny and I and the two-wheeled anathema all came to a screeching halt in one pile. Despite our extended slide down the blacktop, we sustained no injuries other than a red spot on my right ankle, but the incident planted in me a seed of dislike for that particular piece of machinery. For a number of years, I never told my father of that episode. By the time I did tell him, he had already found out for himself that the conventional motorcycle was a much safer vehicle.

Dad looked through the phone book and gave Roland Free, the Indian motorcycle dealer in Indianapolis, a call. Rolly came out with a 1937 Indian 30-cu.in. Junior Scout. After riding the Scout, Dad and I rationalized that this vehicle was much superior to the Cushman and would better suit our needs on our collection route. As I look back, I don't know who was kidding whom. My mother was less than enthusiastic about the whole deal but had the wisdom to hold her tongue. Her youngest brother rode motorcycles, and I think she took the attitude that boys will be boys, regardless of their age.

Rolly took me down a side street, explained how the throttle and front and rear brakes worked, then turned me loose. I picked up on riding pretty quickly and when we returned to the store, Rolly commented to Dad, *"You won't have any problems with him, he looks like a natural-born rider!"* I decided right then that I wanted my own Junior Scout. In actuality, these bikes were not very safe, as they had a peculiar trait of going into a speed wobble when changing gears, but they were state-of-the-art back then. I did eventually get my own.

I recall one hot and sultry evening, when I rode to Maywood, Indiana on my new Junior Scout. Maywood is where the infamous outlaw, John Dillinger, hailed from. Although I never knew Dillinger, his sister and brother-in-law and some nieces and nephews were friends of mine. Anyway, folks were sitting in front of their homes in swings and lawn chairs when I pulled up in front of Don Winings' house. *"Hey, Don, I wanna show you a new stunt I just learned to do on my Indian!"* I hollered. I was confident that I could pull this off, as I had already practiced it a few times without incident. I rode down the street about two blocks, turned around and got the Junior Scout up to about thirty miles an hour. Then I stood upright on the saddle and let go of the handlebars. Instantly, I felt that something was wrong. I didn't have my balance just right - maybe my concentration wasn't as great in front of onlookers - but I fell off the bike. I tried to hit the ground running, but went head first instead and plowed a 30-foot-long furrow with my face! Whee, that hurt like crazy! When I was able to get up, I limped over to the bike and turned off the wildly running engine, then headed back to the house to eat crow. I couldn't just have done this embarrassing stunt in front of my buddy. Oh, no. I had to do it in front of half the town! One old guy wise-cracked, *"I seen that tried before, sonny, but I never seen it work so well!"* I did, however, survive to become a fairly good rider, entering a number of endurance and off-road races in later years.

Anyhow, Dad and I rode the slightly unwieldy Junior Scouts for nearly three years before we both got a yearning for the bigger, newer bikes that were becoming available. I bought a new 1940 45-cu.in. Indian Scout, complete with trumpet-shaped horns. Naturally, Dad would not be outdone, so he bought a slightly used Indian 74. We still had one Junior Scout we had kept for our collection route and one summer I ran it in the annual Hare and

23

Hound Cross-Country Race. I placed fourth and managed to keep it rubber side down most of the race!

Shortly after having been bitten by the motorcycle bug, I joined the Indianapolis Motorcycle Club which had its headquarters at 344 North Delaware Street. Rolly Free was a member and the club was comprised largely of older, more mature riders. In a couple of years, however, I was elected president of the Club. Our meetings were held each Wednesday night, after which we would usually take a ride to some nearby small town for a soft drink or ice cream before heading back to Indianapolis.

After one of these ice cream runs down to Mooresville, several of us younger guys ended up racing back to town. Now, even in the daylight this was a bit foolish to attempt on those winding back roads. At night - well, I'll just say that we were really taking our chances. Pete Fisher and Berkeley Peck had super high-performance Indian Chiefs. I was leading the group out of town with my 45-cu.in. Indian Scout, all tucked in and doing about ninety miles an hour, when Pete and Peck flew by me on their Chiefs like I was standing still. I looked back to check if anyone else was approaching on my tail - and my glasses blew right off my face! Well, without glasses I might as well have been driving by Braille. I grabbed my front and rear brake levers and brought the bike to a stop as quickly as I could. Several of the riders stopped to see if I had mechanical trouble. I told them what had happened and we started walking up and down the ditches looking for my specs - or at least what was left of them. Several more of my buddies pulled up and joined in the search. About 500 yards back, just when I was about to give up, I spotted the glasses lying right on the center line of the road, unbroken. I thanked Providence that a big truck hadn't happened along within the past twenty minutes or so!

The motorcycle club seemed to be divided into two age groups: guys eighteen to twenty years of age, and another group in the thirty to 35-year range. Bob Sheets, Emory Turner and I had all graduated from Ben Davis High School and got the motorcycle fever about the same time. We met two other riders in the club who were our age, Floyd Breedlove and Herman Trout. Both of them had attended the Zionsville High School. They lived about seventeen or eighteen miles from us. We used to go on club rides to various races around Indiana and surrounding states, as well as cover just about every square inch of highway within a 500-mile radius of Indianapolis.

The Indianapolis Motorcycle Club frequently held its own club functions, especially in the spring and fall. We always looked forward to the national flat-track racing event in Springfield, Illinois. One of our more unconventional riders was Oliver Levergn Brown. He was older than my usual riding buddies, but he and his wife, Frances, were interesting people. Levergn once rode a motorcycle from the Pacific to the Atlantic Ocean in just one hour. I guess this one's kind of tough to figure out, unless you know that he was in Panama and that it's only sixty miles from one side of the Isthmus to the other! He also built one of the first workable motorcycle camping trailers I ever saw.

A bunch of us were riding down in Kentucky one time when my buddy, Emory Turner, met with a slight mishap. It was after dark and I was counting headlights in my mirror just to make sure we were still all together. I came up one headlight short. I stopped the other guys and we sat there for a few minutes before deciding to turn back and look for our missing buddy. About two miles back, we saw a single flashing light down over the embankment. Emory had taken that last corner a little too fast, gone off the road and over the bank, ending up in the yard next to a little cabin. The old guy who lived there heard the racket and came out to investigate. He found Emory with the bike on top of him and the motor still running. I can imagine what he thought. Other than a bruised ego, and a few scratches on his bike, Emory was in fine shape.

On Saturday afternoons, the guys with the Harleys and Indians would sometimes get together to find out just who had the "hottest iron." The riders wanted to maintain some degree of safety during these runs, so South Harding Street would be cordoned off and automobiles were detoured elsewhere. I don't recall many of the bikes the guys raced, but I distinctly remember that Berkeley Peck owned an Indian that, to use Rolly Free's expression, really "pruned" the 74-cu.in. Harley-Davidson. It was a beauty. Somehow, the cops always found out about these street drags and came out to break them up. Everyone managed to scatter quickly as they arrived, so no one was ever arrested. I imagine an irate neighbor may have tipped them off; those big bike engines can get pretty loud when they're wrapped up all the way!

I was usually an observer at these races, my 45 not having the juice it took to make a showing. I did, however, inadvertently become a participant in a drag race on Indiana State Road 67. I was cruising along on my Scout at about fifty miles an hour when an Indian 74, a Harley 61, and a 1940 Ford coupe nearly blew me off the road. They stopped up ahead at the small village of Camby and I asked them who had won the race. Apparently the Indian and the Ford ran neck and neck, so they were going to settle the tie by racing back to Valley Mills, whence they had come. My 45 Indian Scout was strictly stock except for some of Rolly's fine-tuning. I decided to join the group and see if I could possibly make a showing against any of them. I had never run against a 61 Harley and figured I didn't have a chance. The 74 Indian was supposedly a Bonneville, and the Ford owner said he had a modified engine and a Columbia rear end. I didn't hold out much hope for making a showing against any of them. Once we got under way, though, even running the smallest engine, I soon passed the 61 Harley. I think a lot of my speed was due to my ability to tuck in and hence become more aerodynamic than the other guy on the bigger machine. Before long, I realized that I was holding my own against the Ford and the Indian Chief! Later, after some discussion, I realized the Ford and the 74 weren't really as hopped-up as I had been led to believe and that the rear end in the Ford was probably just stock. Even so, we all concurred that our speedometers had registered between 95 and 100 mph.

Harley-Davidson always sold more motorcycles than the Indian Company but, in my opinion, Harley did not necessarily build a better product. An Indian 45 right out of the crate would outrun the Harley 45 by at least ten miles an hour. A Harley 61-cu.in. would run about 95 mph, just about the same speed as the smaller Indian 45. Over the years, I owned several of the big Harleys, but the vibration of the engine would get so bad that the speedometer would just go crazy. In most V-twin engines, whether automobile or motorcycle engines, the two cylinders rarely oppose each other by exactly 45 degrees. The Indian was a 42-degree design; the British Vincent a 50-degree. The Harley was the only one I know of where the

26

cylinders were at a 45-degree angle to each other, and it increased the engine vibration considerably. I sold my standard 45-cu.in. Indian just before I entered the service. It had 41,000 trouble-free miles on it.

Rolly Free, the Indian motorcycle dealer, was born to race. In addition to trying his hand at auto racing in the Indianapolis 500 several years in a row, he set many speed records on motorcycles. He had established a number of records with 45-cu.in. Indian Scouts as well as on the larger 74-cu.in. Indian Chief. But the Indian motorcycle company was about to close its doors, so the 61-cu.in. British Vincent became his next passion. Rolly set a speed record of 150 mph riding one of the Vincents. In earlier years, Rolly had set records with Indians at the Daytona Beach track. Later, his racing records were set at the Bonneville Salt Flats in Utah. Shortly after setting the 150-mph record, he set another at 160 mph. Rolly and his sponsor fabricated a special shell which encased the bike and served to streamline it. After that modification, the Vincent was unofficially clocked at 180 mph. When Rolly went to time the bike officially, however, he had exceeded 180 mph when the shell suddenly split apart and the bike went down, sliding some one thousand feet. By the time Rolly quit sliding, much of the skin was gone from his back. He would have bled profusely had the salt from the track not been rubbed into the raw skin, stanching the bleeding. This little episode sounded the death knell on Rolly's motorcycle speed record attempts. His wife, Margie, told him, *"Rolly, I've put up with your shenanigans for a long time, but this is it. Either the motorcycles go or I go!"* Well, for me, that would've been a pretty tough choice, but Rolly just muttered something about it being too much trouble to break in a new wife, and gave up motorcycle racing for good.

Red Davidson, one of the early motorcycle cops in Indianapolis, was a colorful figure. I was coming home from work one day on my Indian Scout when I saw a motorcycle cop coming up behind me. As soon as he pulled alongside, I realized who it was. Now, Red disliked Indian motorcycles, but the city had recently elected to buy 4-cylinder Indians for the police force and the poor guy had no choice but to ride a brand-new Indian 4. Anyway, Red yelled over at me, *"Hey, crank that Scout up and let's see what it'll do!"* I was afraid he was baiting me into getting a ticket, but he insisted that we have a little race. We took off through a 30-mph zone at about 65 or 70 mph and he easily pulled away from me. I was impressed. Then he took me over to his house where we talked motorcycles and he even ended up giving me some new spark plugs which were probably courtesy of the Indianapolis Police Department. Red and Cannonball Baker, the transcontinental motorcycle and automobile record holder, lived near each other in Indianapolis. Red Davidson lived on West Minnesota Street, and "Bake" lived on the south side in a place called Garfield Park, about four miles away. Cannonball Baker began making transcontinental runs as early as a few years before World War II. He ended his career with more than 150 record runs. Most of these were from Los Angeles to New York City, but he also made quite a few north to south runs from Blaine, Washington to Tijuana, Mexico.

Another interesting character in the Indianapolis area was the legendary Floyd "Pop" Dreyer who, thanks to his experience in the military service, became an excellent motorcycle sidecar racer. He developed a special linkage that allowed the sidecar to lean with the motorcycle, enabling the rider to go much faster on curves. His creation was dubbed the "Flexy". The Flexy soon became a popular sidecar for regular highway travel. Floyd worked for a while as a welder for the Duesenbergs and helped build the Stutz Blackhawk, which set a land speed record at Daytona Beach in 1928. In the 1930s, Floyd built some very fast cars for dirt track racing. Duke Nalon, a former 500-mile racer set several half-mile records with the Dreyer 4-cylinder engine. One year, Floyd built the bodies for all three of the racers in the front row of the Indy 500. In 1959, he opened a Honda motorcycle dealership, the first one east of the Mississippi, and his son still operates that same dealership today. Pop Dreyer died in 1989 at age ninety. He had just quit riding motorcycles the previous year.

One thrill-seeker whose passions included motorcycle competition was Charles Lindbergh, the famous aviator. I will never forget the morning my dad took me to the airport to watch Charles Lindbergh land. He had just flown the Spirit of St. Louis across the Atlantic a few months before. I was only eight at the time, but I still remember the thrill and excitement the crowd felt when he brought that remarkable aircraft in. Anyway, Lindbergh cut quite the figure on his Excelsior Super X. The Excelsior motorcycle company folded very quickly, despite producing some of the best hill-climbing machines ever built.

There were many talented and gutsy motorcyclists and motorcycle racers in that era who deserve mention and, unfortunately, that is about all they're going to get in this chapter. I wish I had been able to devote more time and attention to them, as each has his own fascinating story. There was Joe Petrali, the dyed-in-the-wool Harley-Davidson buff who excelled in road racing, hill climbing and setting drag racing records and who, interestingly enough, also co-piloted Howard Hughes' famous Spruce Goose. And Jim Davis, who officiated at almost every Daytona Beach motorcycle race and National Championship race in the 1940s. Jim was even hit once by a motorcycle as he was on the track handing the flag to the winner for the victory lap!

CHAPTER THREE

HOT CARS, HOTSHOT MECHANICS
AND OLD, BOLD PILOTS

Having been raised in Indianapolis and living less than three miles from the famous Indy 500 racetrack, I got to rub elbows with a few well-known people involved in building and distributing exotic passenger cars and racing vehicles. Even today, it's not uncommon to hear the complimentary phrase, *"What a doozie!"* This was an expression derived from the exceptional automobile built by August and Frederick Duesenberg. Augie was a

August and Frederick Duesenberg, 1920s

customer of mine in later years, when I owned a hardware store on the west side of Indianapolis. Fred Duesenberg eventually died in one of his own sedans on a road somewhere in Pennsylvania. Augie died much later, with hardly a penny to his name. His 1927 Duesenberg sedan remains on display in the Indianapolis 500 Museum in Speedway City, Indiana.

The Depression had devastated even the wealthy, and many of the owners of exotic race cars could not find sponsors. There were even some competitors who couldn't afford a pair of racing goggles and had to borrow them. Engine displacement specifications were increased to allow the use of less expensive, conventional passenger car engines. Rolly Free took advantage of this trend and entered his 1929 eight-cylinder Chrysler roadster in the Indy 500. He had to make numerous modifications and ran into snags in achieving the correct gear ratios suitable for racing, so he compensated by putting oversized tires on the roadster. His theory worked and he was able to qualify the semi-stock roadster for the 1930 Indianapolis 500. It was common practice for a mechanic to ride shotgun and Tom Kafouri was Rolly's riding mechanic. The Chrysler held its own against the more sophisticated racers until about halfway through the race, when it developed insurmountable problems which put Rolly and Tom out of it.

Rolly Free, 1930

I recall the time Ray Stearns, a riding mechanic, went for an unauthorized joyride in a Duesenberg racer. No one had yet been chosen to drive the Doozie in the race. Several drivers had demonstrated their abilities, but not to the satisfaction of the owners. Ray's job was to start the car and warm up its engine. He performed that task admirably - and then some. Apparently, he decided that there was no reason he shouldn't be given a chance to drive the car in the race, so he threw the engine crank into the cockpit and took off! The owners ran out onto the track and tried to flag him down, but he ignored them and managed to get four fast laps in before his conscience got the better of him. He received a good tongue lashing, but he swore it was well worth it.

Ray Stearns, 1930

During World War II, Rolly Free went into the Air Force as a major. Ford Moyer, who had an automobile repair shop close to Rolly's motorcycle shop, was able to locate the old front drive Miller Special, dubbed the Bristow-McManus Special, that Fred Frame had driven to victory in the 1932 Indianapolis 500. Rolly Free would have a fairly competitive race car to run in the first race after he came home from the war.

The vintage racer made a good showing until, once more, mechanical problems put Rolly out halfway through the race. Undaunted, the crew tried again the following year, still running that old 1932. About 150 miles into the race, the engine locked up and sent the old car into a grinding skid in the number one turn, throwing Rolly out of the race for a third time. I saw him the following day and noticed he was limping a little. I asked him how he had hurt himself. *"After getting myself extricated from the cockpit,"* he said dryly, *"the left rear wheel rolled forward and ran over my right foot!"* That was the last time that old Miller Front Drive ever raced in the Indianapolis 500, but it can still be seen in the Indianapolis 500 Museum in Speedway City.

One morning, Cannon Ball Baker drove up while a bunch of us were hanging around the local motorcycle shop. He said he had been experimenting with an older Nash six-cylinder sedan and had built a special carburetor which gave considerably better gas mileage than stock carbs. My skepticism must have been apparent, because he raised the hood and showed me a few external modifications on the Nash. I wasn't too well acquainted with Nashes, so it didn't mean much to me. He did run a 200-degree thermostat, which he claimed increased the mileage. He also ran 100 pounds of air pressure in each tire! But when he showed me a one-gallon jug up in the passenger compartment, I became interested. It had a couple of valves that he could manually turn on and off to adjust fuel flow while driving down the highway. I don't know how the darn thing worked, but with it the Nash could get sixty miles to the gallon! Cannon Ball was getting long in the tooth even then and I guess he ran out of time before he could patent his "carburetor" or whatever it was, so he never got it on the market.

RACING TIME

with

CANNON BALL BAKER

About nine years after I experienced the excitement of Lindbergh's landing in Indiana, I got the opportunity to fly in an airplane with one of the great racing pilots of that era. Roscoe Turner flew in the Thompson Trophy Air Races in Cleveland, Ohio, and won the competition at least three times. His plane was quite small and mostly engine. The Gilmour Oil Company sponsored Roscoe, who sometimes flew with a lion sitting in the rear seat as an advertising gimmick. I was about sixteen or seventeen, and I didn't really frequent airports then, as I was pretty busy with my nose in the wind, but I happened to be at the Indianapolis Municipal Airport one Sunday afternoon.

Roscoe was taking passengers on 30-minute flights over the downtown Indianapolis area for a fee of $3.75 apiece. The plane was a Lockheed Electra with about an eight- to ten-passenger capacity. Roscoe made Indianapolis his home base and I often saw him driving around town in his 1934 Packard Phaeton. He was a snappy dresser: jodhpurs, riding boots, a fancy pilot's cap and neatly-trimmed, waxed moustache.

It takes the strongest tires made to withstand the terrific impact of a high-speed landing. That's why I use Firestone Tires on my racing planes and on my automobiles.

Roscoe Turner

Only 4-time winner of Thompson Trophy Race and holder of more air speed records than any other pilot in the world

Roscoe Turner in a tire ad, 1930s

Indianapolis 500 racer Wilbur Shaw not only flew airplanes but also taught flying. Ironically, he later died in a weather-related flying accident while returning to Indianapolis from Michigan.

John Hoffman, an old schoolmate of mine, took some flying lessons after he had served in the military. I didn't know that he was not yet licensed when he called me to see if I would like to accompany him to Fulton, Missouri, near St. Louis. It sounded like fun, so I took him up on it. Well, as we neared St. Louis, he called the tower for permission to land. *"Come in behind the Connie,"* instructed the tower personnel, referring to a Constellation, a much larger aircraft which was landing just ahead of us. We did as we were told, but came very close to being slammed to the ground in the turbulence the Constellation had created! Our little plane reared up, then slipped off to the left, but John apparently did all the right things and was able to bring it in under control.

Levergn Brown, my old motorcycle riding buddy, was also a "weekend pilot." He gave me the second flight of my life and many thereafter. He was a very safe, comfortable pilot to fly with and I was always relaxed when flying with him. He and his wife, Frances, once flew from Miami to Havana and then across the Gulf of Mexico to Merida, Mexico and on down to Acapulco in a Cessna 120. Levergn was a Seventh Day Adventist. One day, he was contacted by a member of the church who asked if he was qualified to rebuild a small plane which had crashed in a Mexican jungle. He accepted the mission and was flown in to the short, primitive landing strip near where the plane had gone down. Since there was no electricity in the tiny nearby village, he took only hand tools with him and succeeded in rebuilding the plane in about six weeks. The necessary repairs were extensive; in fact, it turned out the plane was damaged much worse than he had been led to believe. With his limited tools and an abundance of prayer, he began to perform some seemingly impossible feats. A new prop was flown in, along with other major parts. Once he was able to fire up the engine, Levergn spent another two or three days making runs up and down the dirt airstrip until he felt confident enough to take off and head for McAllen Airport in Houston. The airport had been alerted that Levergn was on his way in the derelict plane and gave him clearance to land on one of the strips used exclusively for disabled aircraft. After Levergn made his characteristically smooth landing, the airport officials checked the plane out and gave him the go-ahead to fly on to Fort Lauderdale, Florida. Levergn made frequent stops to check the bird out, but his "shade-tree mechanic" work held up. It wasn't a mechanical problem that finally posed a danger toward the end of the trip;

rather, it was an exhausted fuel supply within sight of the airport! Undaunted, Levergn immediately began spinning the prop with the battery to reduce wind drag and cleared the fence at the end of the runway. I imagine he landed without so much as a bump.

Another of my motorcycle riding partners, Berkeley Peck, was also a pilot. One Sunday afternoon, Berkeley was out flying his Cub, a small, light plane without much horsepower. He was flying over Sixteenth Street which was about sixteen blocks from the 300-foot-tall Soldier and Sailor's Monument in Indianapolis. He banked right and was headed in the direction of the monument when he realized he was bucking a strong headwind. The end result was that it took Berkeley thirty minutes to pass over the Soldier and Sailor's Monument! I'll bet he could have set a world record for flying in place.

CHAPTER FOUR

WESTWARD HO!

By the early 1940s, many of the members of the Indianapolis Motorcycle Club had entered the armed services. Bob Sheets entered the Navy and was stationed in San Diego. Emory Turner was in the Army in Virginia and ended up in Persia (now Iran) for two years. Our Indian 4 rider, Herman Trout, was also in the Army.

Neither Floyd Breedlove nor I had ever been west of the Mississippi River, so we decided to make the trip before we got drafted, since we would soon be called up. Floyd had a beautiful 1941 4-cylinder Indian and I had a 1940 Indian Sport Scout. Both bikes were just perfect for the trip. To the best of my recollection, we each had just a little over two hundred dollars. Gasoline was twelve to sixteen cents per gallon and motels were around three bucks a night. Camping out cut our travel expenses considerably. Because of the war, tires were already becoming hard to obtain, so we decided to keep our speed down to 50 mph to conserve rubber. Since we were eligible for the draft, we had to obtain permission from the draft board for our western junket.

We left Indianapolis about 5:00 o'clock in the morning and by the end of the first day had made it halfway through Arkansas. It looked like a storm was coming, so we splurged for a three-dollar motel room. When we got back on the road the next day, the dark, greenish clouds seemed to follow us. Just east of Texarkana, the storm, which had worked itself into a tornado, caught up with us. Living in Indiana, we knew the signs and immediately ran our bikes into a borrow ditch and lay down flat. It was none too soon, because that tornado ripped through an area about a mile away from us, causing considerable damage.

The nearly 1,000-mile journey across Texas seemed to take forever. We did get a break in the monotony when we stopped for gasoline in Sweetwater. Both of us had to go the restroom. We were anxious to get rolling again and wasted no time in firing up the bikes and getting under way. We had gone about forty miles when Floyd pulled up beside me and said, *"Hey, I forgot to pay for that gasoline back there!"* So he rode all the way back to Sweetwater and rectified his mistake. The operators of the station had realized what had happened shortly after we'd left, but couldn't catch us. Just what we needed. As if it weren't taking us long enough to get across that enormous state, Floyd had to backtrack and repeat part of the trip!

Pretty soon we got into country that looked more like "the West" we had always envisioned. We pulled into Van Horn, Texas, a rustic little place with Spanish-style buildings. We decided we owed ourselves the luxury of a motel room and the gas station attendant recommended a nice little adobe hotel about two blocks down the street. There was a restaurant, so we had an excellent meal for about fifty cents. In those days, tipping was an accepted, but not expected, practice. We slept later than usual the following morning and had breakfast in the hotel's cafe before departing for El Paso.

We had read articles in various motorcycle magazines about a renowned dealer in El Paso. Walt Lupton was reputed to be a specialist in making Indian motorcycles practically fly. You must remember that this was in the spring of 1942, and very few motorcycles could run 100 mph. I mean an honest 100 mph, not a speedometer 100 mph. We lost no time in finding a phone book and looked up Walt Lupton. As El Paso was a small town in those days, it was easy to locate Walt's neat little shop. Sitting out in front was one of those 1940 Indian Chiefs that looked like it was doing 90 mph while sitting on the kickstand. Walt must have seen us coming down the street, because he came out to greet us right away. After introductions, we related the highlights of our trip up to that point. When we mentioned Rolly Free, our Indian dealer and mentor, we were in like Flynn. Of course, Rolly had already broken many Class "C" records on Daytona Beach and had driven in the 1930 Indy 500. As it turned out, Walt was the Texas version of Rolly Free.

Lupton's Indian Sales Company

Well, we sat and exchanged stories for quite a while, which paved the way for each of us to climb aboard that potent Chief sitting out there in front of Walt's shop. After each of us had straddled the bike, Walt said wryly, *"I suppose you boys'd like to try 'er out?"* Four-speed Indians were a rarity then and both of us jumped at the chance. I don't know about Floyd, but I know I never got out of second gear even though I was probably running 80 mph down a city street!

Reluctantly, we said goodbye to our new friend. Our next stop was supposed to be someplace northwest of Lordsburg, New Mexico. It was dark when we finally pulled off into the desert and crawled into our sleeping bags, and we had no idea that we had camped no more than twenty feet from a railroad. At about 2:00 in the morning, we were scared out of our wits when a high-speed passenger train came roaring by! I guess we should count ourselves lucky by twenty feet - we could have camped right in the middle of the darn track, we were so tired! Shortly before the sun came up, we heard, off in the distance, the sound of a motorcycle. It had the unmistakable pitch of a 61-cu.in. Harley and was coming our way. In a few minutes, the rider pulled up at our campsite, got off, and began chatting away like we were long-lost buddies. *"I stopped for gas several days ago in Arkansas and they told me you guys had gassed up there about an hour before I pulled in,"* he said. *"Everywhere I stopped to gas up, I'd get the same story!"* So he had decided to get an early start that day and try to catch up with us. He was from Pennsylvania and headed for Los Angeles. We rode together almost as far as Phoenix, where Floyd and I took our leave and turned southwest toward Yuma, Arizona.

I was running a few minutes ahead of Floyd when we arrived in Globe, Arizona, outside of Phoenix. I can recall the episode like it occurred yesterday. I had just passed through a traffic signal when I noticed a nice-looking gal walking toward me. I stopped, since it was obvious she wanted to talk to me. Immediately I could tell she had been hitting the sauce. *"Oh, that's a pretty motorcycle. Will you take me for a ride?"* she said, with a somewhat slurred speech.

"Uh, n-no," I stuttered, petrified. Girls were not my area of expertise, especially ones who seemed a little tipsy. *"I'm not a very good rider, but my friend is coming into town in a few minutes and he's a real good rider. He even likes girls!"* By that time I saw Floyd coming and I flagged him over and told him this girl wanted to take a ride with him. Old Floyd, of course, didn't mind at all. He gave her a short ride, she was effusively grateful, and Floyd never even caught on that she was soused.

We toured on in to the big city of Phoenix which probably had a population of about 40,000 at that time. We ate lunch and when we came out of the restaurant, we saw that our motorcycles were completely surrounded by fascinated people, many of whom had never even seen a motorcycle before.

We had heard that there was an agricultural inspection station set up just west of Yuma, but since the food we had on board was limited to mostly fruit, we didn't think there would be any problem. We had absolutely no idea then that many fruits from out-of-state areas harbored insects injurious to California flora and that the state had very stringent regulations governing what could be taken across the border. As I recall, we passed inspection okay and continued on into California.

The Algodones Sand Dunes just west of Yuma were very interesting. Much of the old wooden plank road that early motorists used to get to San Diego still existed. We were getting tired after a very long day and chose a lonely but peaceful stretch of desert about twenty miles into California as our campsite that evening.

The following morning, we decided to see if we could find a place where we could cross over into Mexico. We located a sleepy little town called Jacumba, where there was a sign indicating that it was possible to cross the border here, but that permission to pass through the gate could be revoked at any time. We went through the gate just so we could tell the folks back home that we had been in Mexico, but we didn't dally for long. That sign kind of gave us the willies; besides, we wanted to get on up to the San Diego Naval Base and see our old motorcycling buddy, Bob Sheets.

We found Bob and, luckily enough, he was off duty for a while. He suggested that we go to Old Town and secure a room first, then take in the sights. We followed his advice and were able to get a fairly nice room for our usual three bucks per night. When we went back to the base to get Bob, however, it turned out he couldn't get off duty after all. So we took a quick tour of the base and spent the next couple of days looking around San Diego. We could hardly wait to go swimming in the Pacific Ocean but found the water much colder than we anticipated. Thinking back, the locals must have found us very amusing because we positively fractured the names of streets and towns, having never been familiar with Spanish pronunciation. You can imagine what we did to names like La Jolla, which is supposed to be pronounced "La Hoya."

All too soon, we had to say goodbye to our buddy, Bob, and head north to Los Angeles. When we arrived and checked in at a hotel, we learned that motorcycle short-track races were being run nearby that evening. I had read about these races, but hadn't ever seen any in Indiana. Floyd and I decided this would be a good way to spend the evening. Robert Stack, a young movie star, was to be the honorary starter for the races. We hit pay dirt that evening, because the best short-track racers in the world, Jack Milne and his brother Corky, were there. When the evening was over, we considered it money well spent. The following day we checked out Hollywood. We were observing a highly-modified Buick coupe at one of the studios when its owner came out. Bill Marshall had appeared in several movies we had seen and we recognized him at once.

The motorcycles were overdue for some preventive maintenance, especially oil changes. We headed for Johnson Motors, a place we knew sold and serviced Indian motorcycles. We had heard a lot about this place before and hoped to see our racing hero, Ed Kretz, who owned the shop. Not only did we get to see Ed, but he personally worked on our bikes. A strange thing occurred as we were killing time there. Another young fellow came riding up to the shop on his Indian. It turned out that a year before, almost to the very day, I had met and talked with him in Rolly Free's Indian shop back in Indianapolis! It was just before the Indy 500 and he was there to see the race.

We spent one more day just riding around downtown Los Angeles and nearby coastal areas. Our funds were beginning to dwindle, so we decided to leave the big city and look for an inexpensive motel northeast of Los Angeles. The following morning, we rode the bikes up through Cajon Pass. This was our first major climb since leaving western New Mexico at an elevation of slightly over 4,000 feet. The road at that time was just two lanes wide, as opposed to its present four or five lanes each direction. We ate breakfast in Victorville and then headed for the busy old railroad town of Barstow and its neighboring ghost town of Calico. We experienced our first real heat as we approached Baker, with its numerous dry lakes. We drank several bottles of soft drinks to quench our thirst before heading up the highway to the California-Nevada state line. Evaporative coolers for automobiles could be rented at some gas stations for the drive over the pass, then dropped off at another station near Las Vegas where the deposit would be returned. These were the precursors to air conditioners, which appeared shortly after World War II.

I would hazard a guess that the population of Las Vegas in 1942 was about 35,000. The town, or at least the gambling section, was in what they now call the "old" part of town. This is where the Plaza Hotel was located. Playing the penny and nickel slots was the extent of my gambling and when I got ahead by almost four dollars, I quit. We ate a late breakfast with part of our winnings, then headed out to Lake Mead and Boulder (now Hoover) Dam. This was our first experience with hot desert weather and we rode our motorcycles right up to the water's edge. I jumped off the bike and ran right into the water, boots and all. I could see nothing about this desert country that I liked and if someone had told me then that I would one day love living in the desert, I'd have told him he was nuts. Remember, this was in May. In another month or so, the temperature would be well over 100 degrees.

We never did make it out to the dam that trip, but spent some time chatting with a young lady named Ruth Peel, who worked in a refreshment stand by the lake. I got Ruth's address and corresponded with her until I got out of the Army in 1946.

Floyd and I returned to Las Vegas, then turned northeast toward Utah. It was dark, and few cars were on the road. It had cooled down drastically from the heat of the day. I still wasn't impressed by what I had seen of the desert but, to be fair, driving through in the dark is not the best way to determine how nice an area is. I later discovered that southern Utah is one of the most beautiful places on Earth. We passed within twenty miles of Zion National Park and, later, almost as close to Bryce. We didn't take the time to visit either of these marvelous spots and I'll always regret it, even though I've seen plenty of both of them since. All we were doing was seeing how many miles we could cover.

That night, we camped somewhere near Cedar City, Utah. We ate breakfast at a little cafe in the small town of Parowan, just north of Cedar City. We had spotted an Indian motorcycle with a sidecar parked out in front. We got to chatting with the rider and learned he was from Toledo, Ohio and was headed home as he was also anticipating being drafted soon. He wasn't going through Salt Lake City, as we were, but we enjoyed riding with him for the next 130 miles.

The weather was perfect. We pulled into Salt Lake City and found a nice motel for around three dollars. We were carrying our share of road grime and were looking forward to putting it down the drain. The Tabernacle had been highly touted, so we had already put it on the top of our list of places to visit the following morning. Despite being a large city, Salt Lake seemed to be extremely quiet and we slept very well that night. We enjoyed our visit to the Tabernacle and the Mormon Temple and shot a lot of pictures before heading out to the Great Salt Lake. The first thing we noticed upon our arrival at the lake was the absence of people. Nobody was swimming! Nevertheless, we donned our swimming suits and hit the water. The water was excruciatingly cold and took our breath away, but we really did float, just like the brochures said we would. We agreed that the middle of May was not the best time to swim in the Great Salt Lake, but played around anyway for a while before leaving.

Our schedule dictated that it was time to head east, so with our gas tanks full, we started back, riding the remainder of the day and camping for the night. We took U.S. 40 and it wasn't long before we could see the beautiful Uintah mountains off to the south. At a gas stop, we learned that the

Uintahs were the highest mountain range in Utah. We rode through a quiet little village named Duchesne, which, of course, we pronounced Doo-kez-nee. It was not until years later that I learned it was pronounced Doo-shane. Duchesne borders on Ute Indian reservation land. The Utes were the prevalent tribe in western and central Colorado and northeastern Utah during the late 1800s and early 1900s. We saw fewer and fewer towns on this stretch of the journey; Roosevelt and Vernal were about the last sizable towns we passed through and we were beginning to get a little nervous and anxious to get back to civilization.

Our journey through Colorado was all we hoped it would be, especially the leg of it which took us through the Rocky Mountains. The old mining towns of Craig and Steamboat Springs were steeped in history, and Grand Lake was just as the name implied. We traveled across Rabbit Ears and Berthoud Passes on a gravel road. This was the highest I had ever been and the snow, which was left over from the winter, was still deep.

Denver's population was around 360,000 at that time; it was a very clean town and that impressed me. The motorcycles were still performing perfectly, but we thought it would be wise to check in with Denver's Indian motorcycle dealership. Mike Tagaris, owner of the shop, and his nephew Jimmy, were very helpful and friendly. Mike insisted that we have lunch with him and regaled us with tales of activities along the "Front Range," the eastern slope of the Rocky Mountains. Because of our conversation with Mike, we decided to spend a couple of days exploring the Front Range. Although Mike told us it would not be possible to reach the summit of Pike's Peak, he did not discourage our going as far as we could. We were able to reach the 10,000-foot level where the "Road Closed" sign turned us back. We stayed in Colorado Springs one day and night and then headed for home across the flatlands of eastern Colorado and Kansas.

We had heard of Pop Harding, the oldest Indian Dealer in the United States, so we made it a point to stop at his shop in Topeka, Kansas. He was exactly the gentleman we had heard he was. The remaining 500 miles to Indianapolis were as trouble-free as the previous 5,000.

Uncle Sam had not contacted me yet so, in August, Don Winings and I obtained a one-week permit to go to Niagara Falls on our motorcycles. I had been up there several times before and was able to act as a guide.

CHAPTER FIVE

UNCLE SAM COMES KNOCKING

As expected, I was drafted shortly after the Niagara trip. Fort Harrison, Indiana was my home for a week before I was sent to Valparaiso, Indiana to work at the Dodge Telegraph & Radio Institute. There were fewer than twenty military cadre in this radio school. Private instructors taught enlisted men between thirteen and 26 weeks of code. When I left Fort Harrison, I thought I was going to learn code at the Dodge Institute, but instead, I was dubbed Mail Clerk and given the grade of T-5.

I was thrown in with a bunch of real characters, brilliant guys long on intellect and imagination, but with the attendant oddities one finds along with genius. We were housed in an old Civilian Conservation Corps barracks one mile north of town. Major Parry was the head honcho and he introduced me to the other enlisted men. The major was transferred soon after I arrived and was replaced by a Major Shucker from the Pennsylvania National Guard. They must have brought the guy out of mothballs, because he was downright ancient. The next and only other officer was First Lieutenant Overman. He was Regular Army and looking at retirement soon. All the enlisted men liked him. Sergeant Darys Newman was a likable guy, too, a trait rather uncommon in men of his rank. Like most of us, Sergeant Newman worked in the office. He was from Ohio and chummed around with Corporal Bob Maroney. Bob was another Hoosier and probably the guy with the highest I.Q. in the cadre. Staff Sergeant Jim Nelson was regular Army, but died before the war was over. Corporal Dick Falk, from Willard, Ohio, was one of my closest Army friends. He was an excellent medic and we whiled away many a night chatting. Dick had a deep desire to become a physician.

Newman, Maroney, Falk, Sam Crossland (whom we dubbed "Crow" because he liked to drink Old Crow whiskey) and I were the occupants of one of the barracks but, after a couple of months, we all moved into private homes in town. I lived at 401 North Lincolnway and paid thirty dollars a month in rent. I ate my breakfast at the Hotel Lembke and noticed a very pretty girl who also frequented the restaurant there. In an uncharacteristic moment of forwardness, I introduced myself to her. Her name was Virginia Palonis. I found I liked her very much and, thereafter, timed my breakfast so that I got to eat with her as often as possible. We became great friends and I remember her with fondness.

One day, Darys Newman and another guy chipped in together and bought an old 1926 Whippet two-door sedan. Newman and Crow were touring around downtown Valparaiso on a chilly afternoon, with Newman driving the Whippet. All of a sudden, the steering wheel comes right off the column in Newman's hands! Startled, Newman kind of jerks backwards, still holding the steering wheel. As luck would have it, the back of the seat chooses that moment to give way and Newman keeps right on going, ending up in the back seat with his butt up in the air. Now, Crow, who is in the passenger seat taking in the sights, doesn't notice that his driver is upside down on the rear floorboards. He looks over to say something to Newman. Seeing no one there and thinking the car has stopped and that Newman has got out to look at something, Crow, still doing 20 mph, opens his door and promptly steps out onto his face in the middle of the heavily-traveled thoroughfare. I don't know how either of them made it back from that trip alive, but they did. I suspect the whole affair may have had something to do with that Old Crow whiskey.

Since I was into buying and selling motorcycles, I always kept one or two on hand. I had a few girls that I favored, but Norma and Marge had top billing much of the time. I had been seeing Marge quite frequently, so I decided to take her on an evening ride. We were on the way back from the Indiana Dunes. I had stretched my "ride" a little more than I intended and, twenty miles from Valparaiso, the bike was acting up and I was getting concerned that we may have to walk the last few miles. The 4-cylinder Indian was down to only two and sounded terrible. Being the gearhead that I am, I spent all that time worrying about the bike instead of making the best of the situation. Most guys would have welcomed the excuse of a mechanical breakdown to get stuck out in the sticks with a girl like Marge. Anyway, we limped into town at 2:00 o'clock in the morning. I coasted down the last hill with the key off and as I pulled up to Marge's house, I said in a low voice, *"I hope your mother isn't still up!"* A maternal-sounding voice from behind the bushes said, *"You had better believe it, Buster!"* I don't remember seeing a whole lot of Marge after that.

There were no real military quarters in Valparaiso and, being the only Mail Clerk around, I got extra rations and funds with which to pay the rent. I ended up living in a private home and eating all my meals in restaurants for a year. It could have been worse. I was only 140 miles from my parents' home in Indianapolis and I frequently rode down to visit on weekends.

In the Army, 1943, with 1940 Triumph and friend

As I mentioned, buying and selling motorcycles was a sideline I indulged in. The year I was stationed in Valpo, I bought a 1940 45-cu.in. Indian, sold it and got a 1936 80-cu.in. Harley, sold it and bought a 1939 80-cu.in. Harley. I sold that to Leroy Warriner, an old school chum of mine and the national midget race-car champion. Then I bought the first Triumph Tiger 100 that came to Indianapolis. It was a 1940 model and a real performer. I was its third owner. One weekend, I took a junket into southern Michigan and, on impulse, sold the bike to John Edgar, the Triumph dealer in Grand Rapids, Michigan.

After a year of luxurious living in Valparaiso, I was transferred to Nichols General Hospital in Louisville, Kentucky, where a snafu developed. They didn't need any mail clerks, I had never taken basic training, and I was not skilled as a "ward boy" in a military hospital. Nevertheless, I ended up on night duty, taking care of four wards full of disabled soldiers. I managed, fortunately, to strike a deal with the night corridor sergeant, Jim Taylor, wherein I would cover for him while he took three days off to go to Cincinnati, then I would get three days off to go to Indianapolis. In one year, I managed to get more than 100 days off. I had a beautiful 1941 4-cylinder Indian and could buzz home to Indianapolis in about two hours.

One of the first rides back to Indianapolis turned out to be a spooky affair. It was in early January. Jim Taylor told me I was crazy to attempt a ride to Indianapolis in such extreme cold - and he was right. The midnight weather forecast called for subzero temperatures before daybreak. I had ridden in pretty cold weather before, but never without a windshield. Nevertheless, I went off duty at 7:30 a.m. and headed for the barracks. I put on practically all of the clothing I owned and prepared to go. Motorcycles had no electric starters in those days, so I had to kick it for quite a while to circulate the oil enough to get it to start. By that time I was warmed up, too. It was snowing lightly when I crossed the Ohio River into Jeffersonville, Indiana. My gauntlet gloves were lined with sheepskin, so my hands were warm. About fifty miles south of Indianapolis, the snow quit, but the roads had iced up solid. The few cars on the road were creeping along at a snail's pace. Having done quite a bit of ice skating, I decided the principle was the same, so I cruised on through at about 45 mph, careful not to make any erratic moves. I had twin trumpet horns on the Indian, and I wondered what all those white-knuckled drivers thought about this crazy nut blaring away, passing them on some 2-wheeled contraption. Finally, with only thirty more miles to go, I just had to stop and slap my gloved hands together to restore some circulation. The last fifteen miles seemed the most difficult. I could have sworn that parts of me were about to start dropping off, but I managed to pull into my parents' driveway all in one piece. Norma Jones, a family friend, was there. She happened to look out the kitchen window and yelled, *"Well, for crying out loud! Here comes Frederick Radcliffe on a motorcycle, of all things!"*

I made my first motorcycle sojourn into the Smoky Mountains right after it became a national park in 1938. I was captivated by the beauty of it and made the trip every chance I got. One weekend, I was able to get a 3-day pass and off I went to my beloved Smokies. My itinerary included a circle back through Virginia. This Indian 4 would run an honest 106 mph. The nationwide speed limit was 35 mph. I was running about 60 mph when a Virginia state patrolman pulled alongside in his 1942 Ford 2-door sedan. I quickly dropped back to about 40 mph and he pulled in front of me. So I dropped down a gear and passed him on the left and the race was on! In looking back, I feel a little ashamed of myself for having taken unfair advantage. I knew I had a 20-mph edge on him. Also, in that year, license plates for motorcycles were only four inches long. Even though he had radioed ahead and had an officer sitting on his 61 Harley waiting to get my plate number, the speed at which I was traveling and the small size of the plate made this practically impossible. In a matter of minutes, I had crossed into Bristol, Tennessee, out of their jurisdiction.

In mid-August, I was called in to the main office at the hospital. *"Corporal, we have a man who's being transferred to Washington State and you have been chosen to accompany him to Brigham City, Utah. You interested?"* I asked why he couldn't go by himself and they explained that he had lost his right arm. My job would be to see that he was fed and taken care of on that long train journey. Naturally, I took advantage of what I viewed as a paid vacation. We left Louisville, changed trains in Chicago, and settled in for the 1,500-mile ride to Ogden, Utah. We had our own compartment with bath and other amenities. The poor guy was not feeling too well and skipped several meals on the train. Since we had purchased meal tickets and he often didn't even order, I saved his meal tickets for my return trip. We changed trains in Ogden and got on one bound for Brigham City. It was early morning and I had a bit of a wait before turning around to head back for Louisville. Besides, my train boarded in Ogden. I bid my patient goodbye and good luck, then hitchhiked down to Ogden where I looked up my buddy, Rolly Free, who was now a Major in the Air Force.

Rolly and Margie lived at the Ben Lomond Hotel in Ogden and they insisted in taking me out to dinner. Then Rolly showed me around the military base and even took me aboard a parked B24 bomber. We still had some spare time before my eastbound train arrived and Rolly had his Chrysler coupe there at the base, so he took me out to Farmington and introduced me to some more Indian riders. They had a 1929 Indian 101 Scout and let me ride it. We had so much fun, time literally flew by and I nearly missed my train. We had that Chrysler wrapped up past 80 mph on the return trip and barely beat the train into the Ogden station. I boarded safely and headed back to the old grind.

On the way, the train was delayed due to a heavy rain in Marshall-

Rolly Free with his 1929 Indian 101 Scout

town, Iowa, and the railroad was completely washed out in several places. Thinking ahead, I bought one of the local papers to prove to my superiors that I had a legitimate excuse for being late in returning to the base.

The way things worked out, I didn't have to go through basic training for my first 28 months in the service. I know this was due to some administrative screw-up, but when the war began getting serious, it caught up with me and I was sent to Camp Barkley for basic training. After about four months in Barkley, I, along with others, was called away from maneuvers we were performing about twenty miles from camp and loaded into a troop train. After five days of riding in a rickety old boxcar which had been converted to a sleeper, we arrived at New Dorp, Staten Island, New York. We were assigned bunks pending interviews for reassignment the following day. Those of us guys who would not be interviewed until later were given passes to ride the Staten Island Ferry to the mainland. Many of us went to gawk at downtown Times Square. Two days later, I was sent out to Fort Dupont, Delaware, and ended up a ward boy again for four weeks.

Then things got really tough! I was transferred to the boardwalk at Atlantic City. I lived on the fourteenth story of the Traymore Hotel, which had hot and cold running water and maid service once a week. I worked in Haddon Hall, another luxurious hotel which had been converted to a hospital, and walked half a mile down the boardwalk each morning. Several of us newer guys would wear our swimsuits to work under our hospital whites.

When we went off duty, we would ride the elevator down to the beach and body-surf for about an hour. Then we would walk back up the beach and arrive just in time to clean up and attend dinner in the ballroom at the Traymore. War is hell!

Atlantic City, 1945

During this interval, I had obtained a furlough, traveled to Indiana and ridden my 1939 Indian Chief back to Atlantic City. I got acquainted with quite a few nurses on the amputee ward and when word got out I had a motorcycle, it was easy to get a date. In fact, I remember twice being pulled over by the gendarmes and issued a warning ticket for having two girls on the bike with me. Upon reflection, it was about that time that I started shedding some of my shyness toward the gentler gender.

It seemed I can never learn a lesson easily. One weekend, I headed over to Philadelphia to visit Bob Sheets, who was undergoing some kind of special naval training at a university there. I was coming into Pleasantville, a few miles outside of Philly, at about 50 mph. I saw this motorcycle cop sitting at a nearby station, putting gas in his Harley 61, so I slowed to about 35 mph and hit the first automatic stop sign on the green. I have mentioned that, during the war, speed limits were 35 mph everywhere, even on open highways. I was riding my Chief with a windshield on it. Both automatic signal lights indicated green as I was leaving town. Out of habit, I looked back and, lo and behold, here came the cop on the motorcycle. He was running flat out for all he was worth and that spooked me, even though I was unaware of having done anything wrong - yet. I wicked the throttle and took off. Having a windshield cut down my speed by about 5 mph, allowing me to do only about 90 mph. I began ducking off onto side roads to try to compensate for the speed gain he had on me. The only flaw in this plan was that I didn't know the territory and soon found myself back in the middle of town.

I could see the charges mounting: I was speeding; I had already run two stop signs during the "chase", and was most definitely attempting to evade a police officer. So I made a left turn onto a side street which I belatedly discovered was a dead end. There was a railroad track which ran next to the street; the track itself was up a cinder embankment which I estimated to be about twelve feet high. I knew it was either the railroad or jail. The choice was easy. I gunned it and made it up the steep railroad bed and quickly took off down the track between the rails.

Despite the fact that I had temporarily eluded the officer, he knew the area and I didn't, so I wasn't about to breathe a sigh of relief - yet. By that time, I was committed to a course of action, so I continued along the cinder railroad bed adjacent to the track. I was probably running close to 30 mph and finally, after what seemed an eternity, I approached a sand trail that crossed the railroad. I knew if I took the sand trail to the right, I would come out onto the same road I had turned off of earlier in the chase. Totally unacceptable. That meant I had to go to the left and head for the backwater town of Absecon Bay. I did this and soon found myself in a thick grove of small palmetto-like trees. I pulled deeper into the grove and immediately shut off the engine. For a few minutes I just lay there not knowing what to do. When my ears quit ringing, I could hear the cop's motorcycle going back and forth as he searched for me. Finally, the sound faded, but I lay there a while longer before very carefully venturing back to Atlantic City and parking the bike in an unobtrusive location.

I didn't dare ride it for at least a week. In fact, before I did ride it again, I walked a couple of miles to the Harley Davidson motorcycle shop and told them I'd heard that there had been a chase involving the police and another motorcycle and asked if there was any truth to it. They said that there had been such a chase and that the cops were still looking for the guy. As you might imagine, I was Mr. Low Profile for a while following that incident!

Shortly after the motorcycle episode, I decided that perhaps I should take the bike home and store it, as there was a good chance I would be sent to Europe. I obtained a one-week furlough and left early the next morning. I didn't like the way the Indian's engine was sounding and tried to hold my speed down, at least until I could get into Philadelphia to Gene Shillingford's Indian dealership. I was riding down Huntingpark Avenue in downtown Philly and was paused at a stop sign in my usual obedient manner. When the sign indicated "go," I grabbed a big handful of throttle. Loud, expensive, metallic noises emitted from down deep in that tired old motor. Luckily, it happened just a few blocks from Shillingford's. I walked to the shop and explained my predicament to the mechanic.

Mr. Shillingford came to my rescue and offered me an even trade for a military 30:50 Scout. He certainly didn't have to do that - actually, he had me over a barrel, but he was a decent man and wanted to help. Needless to say, I remain eternally grateful to him. After signing all the necessary papers, I hurriedly switched my license plate over to the smaller bike and headed for the Pennsylvania Turnpike. I had never ridden on a superhighway before. I kept the little Indian down to about 55 mph and she purred along comfortably. I checked a road map and decided to leave the Turnpike before arriving in Pittsburgh. I got off on U.S. 40, which would take me in to Indianapolis via Columbus, Ohio. I arrived in Indianapolis the following day. The furlough went very quickly and, before I knew it, I was on a train headed back to Philadelphia. From there, I rode a bus over to Atlantic City.

CHAPTER SIX

GOODBYE, ATLANTIC CITY

Upon my return from Indianapolis, I learned that I was to be transferred to Camp Edwards near Cape Cod, Massachusetts. Camp Edwards was a staging area for enlisted men being assigned to "liberty ships," vessels which would be returning soldiers from Belgium, now that the war was effectively over. Again, I was appointed Mail Clerk and was relegated to a solitary stint in the mail room. On weekend passes, I would hitchhike out to Cape Cod and board an excursion boat that crossed Massachusetts Bay and landed in Boston. Since it wasn't far, I visited "Bean Town" several times.

Eventually, the odds caught up with me and I was called in to headquarters and informed that I had been assigned a Clerk-Typist position on a European-bound liberty ship. A sergeant met me at the bus station and drove me out to an old factory building in downtown Boston. I climbed the stairs to the third floor, where I was met by still another sergeant who took my records and assigned me to a bunk. There must have been fifty or sixty of us crowded into the dingy, makeshift barracks. The following morning after chow, we fell out for roll call - but my name wasn't read. I wasn't too surprised; I had arrived just hours before and figured my orders hadn't caught up with me yet. After roll call everyone started policing the area, so I dropped in with them and did my share. Over the next few days, I inquired of some of the guys as to life aboard a liberty ship. I seemed to be the only "rookie" boatman; all of the others had made numerous trips to Europe. There was apparently a week or more lay-over time between trips. With the war already over, I was told I would probably only make one trip to Belgium and back.

Every morning, we would fall out for roll call. Every morning, my name wasn't called. The other guys would police the area, then return to their bunks and just lie around or go downtown and catch a movie, so I did what they did. In those days, most movie theaters had a double feature, and I would take in a couple of shows before returning to our old factory building in time for chow. This routine got old after a while, so I decided to ask for a furlough. The sergeant asked my name and, after close and repeated inspections of the records, discovered that there was no such person as me! Later, they found that my orders had slipped down behind a filing cabinet in the office and had never been missed until now! The boat I was supposed to have boarded had not only left for Europe but had already arrived there!

They assured me, however, that there would be another boat. I thought, woefully, that it would be too much to hope for to have my papers get lost again, so I prepared myself for a summons. It came the same day that we got sixteen inches of snow in Boston Commons. I was driven down to the pier and taken aboard the Pierre Soule, the vessel that would be my home for the next thirty days. This liberty ship was manned by Merchant Marines and was capable of twelve knots, or about fourteen miles per hour.

It occurred to me that I still had no idea what my duties were supposed to be on the boat, so I just did what I could to make myself useful. On the second day out, I was asked to go below to the dispensary and make sure everything was battened down, so I secured everything in sight. It was cloudy and dismal as we left Boston harbor, and the snow on the decks was beginning to lose its appeal. Four of us were assigned to a forecastle or, as seaman call it, "fo'c's'le," which is a berth toward the bow of the ship. The ship was lying quite low in the water and I assumed that was normal until I learned that we had 10,000 tons of wheat in the hold.

My first view of England was Land's End, a typical English setting complete with a view of a motor car touring along a country road. This was the last day in 1945, and we steamed through the English Channel with about half the Merchant Marines on board pleasantly liquored up for the occasion.

Once our ship had landed in England, we had to wait for a pilot to take us upriver to Antwerp, Belgium. Since I was a greenhorn, I was the only one of us who didn't immediately get a pass. The Captain assured me, however, that I would receive one the next day. He remained true to his promise, and I had a marvelous time for several days, riding the trolleys and exploring.

One day, when I took a train into Brussels, I observed vast fields of little plants alongside the railroad. I was sitting beside a young man with a German accent and I asked if he knew what the plants were. Grinning at my naivete, he replied that they were Brussels sprouts!

Upon my arrival in Brussels, I located a photo shop and approached a clerk. It was my first encounter with a French-speaking person. My camera was giving me trouble and I had isolated the malfunction, but needed a screwdriver to make the necessary repairs. I did not, however, know the French word for screwdriver. After an interval of frantic gestures and unintelligible grunts, I discovered that a French screwdriver is a "tournevise." I must say that the frustration I experienced in overcoming the communication gap vastly exceeded any difficulty I had in fixing my camera.

Once we made it to Belgium, there were some problems in getting the ship unloaded, so our visit was extended a few days. When the vessel was finally emptied, the ship was moved about one mile downriver. Those of us who had gone in to Antwerp faced several problems when we returned, the most noteworthy of which was locating our ship. The area where it had been moored was a very dark and dismal waterfront. None of our bunch knew any Flemish, and it wouldn't have done us any good anyway, since there wasn't anyone around to ask. Add to this the slight disadvantage of being more than a little inebriated, and - well, you get the picture. It didn't help much that we all had to climb a Jacob's ladder up the side of the ship when we finally found the darned thing. It's a wonder none of us ended up drowning that night!

We didn't depart Antwerp until the 12th or 13th of January. I dropped a bottle containing my name and address into the North Sea at the mouth of the river as we left. One George Shilliam found it ten days later near Peacehaven, England, and wrote me a letter enclosing my note.

The ship held more than 650 men on the return voyage to New York City. The most exciting part of the trip was the fierce storm we encountered about the sixth day out. The ship was listing to the point where I actually thought it might roll over. I made a pendulum, marked it off in degrees, and got a reading of about 36 degrees on one of the wilder lists. Below decks, many of the men's stomachs were listing just as wildly. The Pierre Soule traveled only 75 miles in the 24-hour period during the storm, whereas it would have ordinarily made over 300 miles in fair weather.

Payday came just a couple of days before we pulled into the harbor at New York City. I never saw such a pile of money on a blackjack table in my life. I got sandbagged by a couple of sharpies and lost most of my paycheck before I realized I was way out of my league. Upon our arrival in port, many of us were sent to Fort Hamilton where we spent only a couple of days before the discharge process was completed. From there, a bus took us in to Indianapolis. So ended my estimable military career.

Emory, Martha and Fred, 1945

CHAPTER SEVEN

BACK IN CIVVIES

Like most ex-GIs, I just relaxed for a bit and roamed around looking up old buddies. After about three weeks of that, I began to give some serious thought to going back to work, but where? I had no real practical skills, and nothing I had learned in the military would be useful in civilian life. My dad had sold his furniture store and was in semi-retirement, but he had a friend, Russ Ritchey, who was also in the furniture business. I asked him for a job and was hired on the spot. I worked for Russ for two years. During this time, I courted and married our Baptist Church minister's daughter, Jean.

I had worked in and out of furniture stores since I was twelve years old and felt that I had a pretty good handle on the retail business. I decided that owning a hardware store would be right up my alley. I investigated a very small "Mom-'n-Pop" store out on the west side of Indianapolis. I had saved about $5,000, which was enough to buy the inventory and make a substantial down payment on the property itself. We just barely made a living in the tiny building, but kept telling ourselves that we were gaining worthwhile experience.

Jean, like many women, was anxious to have a baby, and Lois Elaine was born in February of 1950. Being my parents' first grandchild, they were delighted. Fourteen months later, baby Bernard Ray entered the world. I had already experienced a number of sleepless nights with Baby #1 and did not look forward to Baby #2! Of course, the grandparents were ecstatic about this second child, particularly Grandpa since the Radcliffe name would now be perpetuated. These back-to-back births did create some problems at the little hardware store so some part-time employees had to be added to the business. Grandpa was our "extra" when things became too busy.

Dad could see how hard we were trying and came over to our house one night with an offer we couldn't refuse. He suggested that, with his assistance, we erect a larger building on the property and tear down the old one. This turned out to be a winning proposition, and we soon found ourselves the proprietors of a large, successful hardware store.

Over the next dozen years, our business thrived. We employed one full-time worker and a part-time younger lad who worked for a nearby factory and sort of "moonlighted" for us. The residents in our community were in a low- to middle-income group. They performed many of their own household repairs and were excellent customers, as well as good friends to us in many instances. We accommodated them and they, in turn, accommodated us.

As always, I kept my hand in at motorcycle riding and racing during this time. In 1949 and 1953, I entered the 500-mile National Jack Pine Endurance event. In the 1949 event, I quit at the end of the first day because of sheer exhaustion. I was riding the war surplus Indian 30:50 I had traded for back in Philadelphia while I was in the Army. The old Indian was capable of making it at least through the second day, but I was not. In 1953, I moved up to a British AJS bike for the event. Everything was running smoothly until another rider took a nasty fall right in front of me. In attempting to avoid running over him, I hit a big tree. Predictably, this created a serious mechanical disorder to the motorcycle, not to mention causing considerable pain to the driver. I was able to make enough repairs to finish the first 150 miles, but had lost far too many points to hope for a trophy, so I called it a day and dropped out. At this point, I had to admit to myself that, no matter how much I enjoyed it, I was not destined to become a big name in motorcycling.

During the early 1950s, the British Triumph motorcycles were becoming very popular. I heard about a highly modified 650cc Triumph and went out to look it over. I had never ridden a bike as quick as this one, so I bought it. I asked Jean if she would like to go to California for the annual desert motorcycle race to be held near the resort town of Big Bear. She had not been out to California since 1948 and was all for it, especially when I told her that we would take along her Triumph 200 so she could ride around in the desert after the race.

At the 1959 Big Bear race in California

One evening, about two weeks before Christmas, I had closed up the store and was headed home in my car. I had the radio on and Eddie Fisher and I were singing at the top of our lungs when I caught a fleeting glimpse of a headlight to my right. Instantly, there was an impact, and I found myself skidding across the hood of a car. It happened so quickly, and when the dust cleared I could still hear Eddie singing away. I didn't panic because I figured if Eddie could still sing, my car must not be totally destroyed! My glasses were broken, however, and I had a humdinger of a headache. The guy who hit me was a businessman en route to the airport in a rental car. The first person to reach me other than the driver of the car was Dick Schrober, an old high school mate. I asked him to call my wife to come down with the other car. Fortunately, although a little scratched and bruised, I wasn't so seriously injured that we had to cancel our trip to California.

It took about a week to acquire another vehicle for our journey. Chevrolet had just come out with their new 260 cubic-inch V-8, so we bought a two-door wagon and had a hitch mounted on it for pulling a bike trailer.

My buddy, Floyd Breedlove, who had made the first motorcycle trip west with me, lived in San Diego with his wife and three children and we were looking forward to visiting them. Floyd had warned us that some pretty nasty weather was blowing in and suggested that we get out there a day or two early so as to avoid the storm. We made the trip quickly, arriving in the late evening, and got a motel room for the night. The next morning, we awoke to an unprecedented foot of snow on the desert floor!

The starting line of the race was in Lucerne. There were a surprising 550 entries for this cross-country event. Now, I had ridden across the desert back in 1942, but had done so on a paved highway. This was entirely different. I tried not to look too closely at all the big rocks out there on the course. The starting bomb went off right on schedule, but I wasted about three minutes getting my bike fired up. When I finally got moving, I was in kind of an anxiety-induced daze. After about six or seven minutes, I began to do battle with a few of the less-experienced riders, or "culls," as they called them. When I found I could easily outrun some of these riders, I became braver. It was when I overtook a big-name rider and actually passed him that I really got excited.

I had been avoiding what I thought were rocks, but now realized they were really just dry desert plants which I could drive right through with impunity. When I figured this out, I turned up the wick and really poured the coal to that Triumph. Man, I was moving! I couldn't believe it would be so easy! I thought, *"This is like shootin' fish in a barrel!"* Then it happened. See, the plants looked like rocks; conversely, the rocks looked like plants. Well, I launched about ten feet off that first rock. The second one, probably only about five feet. But I tell you, after those two I regained my humility and never passed another name rider in the race.

Two-thirds of the way through, a biker spun out on the trail right in front of me. I piled in on top of him and was thrown off into the snow. The guy who was hot on my trail rode right up my tailpipe and bent a few of the parts on my Triumph. None of us was hurt, although we all three nearly died laughing!

The farther we got into the 150-mile race, the narrower the trail became. My rear brake was gone, the "kill" button was torn off, and the throttle was stuck at about fifteen miles an hour in the lowest gear.

Finally, I came within sight of the finish line, with Aub Labard wait-

ing to check me in. I hoped I would finish far enough ahead to be eligible for a trophy of some kind. I crossed the line, but with my "kill" switch missing, I couldn't shut the bike off. All I could do was shut the fuel petcock off and ride around in circles until the bike ran out of gas. When it finally did, I hopped off and trotted excitedly over to Aub to ask what position I had finished in.

"Hmm. Lemme see. Not too bad - 145th place," he said. Sigh. I guess I was lucky to even get across the finish line, considering all my mechanical problems. I decided just to leave the poor bike there and come back to get it when I had the trailer. I ended up having to push the bike half a mile to get it to the trailer, as the Chevy wouldn't make it to where the bike was parked, due to the snow. By the time I got the doggone thing strapped back on the trailer, my pants were soaked clear through from slipping and falling in the snow, and I had to take them off. Jean held them in front of the car heater while I drove.

Leaving the Lucerne valley, we encountered still another obstacle. Since the snow was highly unusual for southern California, the pass we intended to take was temporarily closed while road crews worked to clear the snow away. We had to wait in the car for quite some time while this was accomplished. In the meantime, a California State Highway Patrol officer walked up to our car to explain the delay and seemed genuinely dumbfounded when he saw me sitting under the wheel with no pants on. I hastened to explain what had happened, although I am still not sure he believed my story.

We returned to Floyd's home in San Diego and spent another night before heading back to Indianapolis. We couldn't resist stopping to take a ride on Jean's Triumph 200 in the Algodones dunes area, along the same route where Floyd and I had seen remnants of the old plank road. I didn't return to compete in the Big Bear Desert Race until 1959. That year, I rode a Harley. I burned a hole in a piston and was out of the race after only forty miles. In 1960, I talked my racer buddies, Mack McClintock and Tony Ford, into entering the Big Bear Race. That year, there were more than 800 bikes competing and the starting line was mass confusion, with engines revving and people yelling. We didn't know it, but several riders jumped the gun and we took off with them, assuming that we simply hadn't heard the starting bomb. We learned when we checked in at the halfway mark that we were disqualified. That was the last time I rode in the Big Bear Race; it was getting too popular and too big to be manageable.

CHAPTER EIGHT

UTAH REVISITED - AGAIN AND AGAIN

Jean was fascinated by Indians so we decided to visit a Navajo reservation on one of our western jaunts. After spending a night in Flagstaff, Arizona, we checked on road and weather conditions to Monument Valley. This was before that stretch of Hwy. 163 was paved, and the road was mostly hard-packed sand. All of our inquiries met with the same answer. The road to Cameron was excellent, but the road to Monument Valley could be very muddy and slippery when wet or snowy. Being fairly young and adventurous, we decided to go at least to Cameron and see how it looked from there.

At last, we arrived in a real Indian town with a real Indian name: Kayenta, Arizona. Many of the homes in the village were real Indian hogans, all with their doors facing east. We drove through Kayenta and soon approached Agathla Peak, the sentinel at the entrance to Monument Valley which covers parts of both Arizona and Utah. Harry Goulding's Trading Post was our prime destination, and we were not disappointed when we arrived. A real Navajo Indian sat on his pony in front of the trading post. We spent hours picking through the artifacts and collectibles. Soon, it was time for lunch, so we drove west up the canyon to find a suitable spot to pull off the trail and eat. We looked in the general direction of Goulding's and saw the same Indian and pony who had been at the trading post heading our way. Jean had read that Navajo etiquette dictated that one invite a visitor to eat, so we made hand gestures asking him to join us. He understood, smiling and nodding, and accepted a portion of our food. He then retreated, with his pony, to a distance of about 20 yards where he sat down and ate his share. When Jean and I were ready to pack up and head for Flagstaff, we gave our new friend an apple which he put in his pocket. Smiling his thanks, he then rode away across the canyon. Half an hour later, as we were traveling back toward Flagstaff, our Indian friend reappeared, crossing the road just ahead of us. He smiled and waved as we disappeared into the west.

Monument Valley itself was an unexpected wonder. Tall buttes and spires of vivid red sandstone towered above the sandy desert floor. The sky was so blue it almost hurt, and Jean and I felt ourselves falling in love with this barren wilderness. We drank it in with our eyes and souls and, when the time came to depart, vowed to return.

9. A. Barnes

The hardware store got along fine without us during our vacation. Of course, we had pictures to show our friends back in Indiana. This introduction to a very unique scenic wonder drew comments from everyone, especially those who had been to nearby Grand Canyon. Many of our hardware customers were amazed that such a place as Monument Valley existed. One customer, however, said, *"Fred, you should have gone on up north another hundred miles to the most beautiful red rock canyons and cliffs you will ever see!"* He went on to say that Moab, Utah, and the surrounding country was the best-kept secret in the southwestern United States. Jean and I found it hard to believe that anything could be more stunning and unusual than Monument Valley, but this new information whet our appetites for more travel and exploration.

Within the year, we took off to check out Moab, Utah, and its surrounding area. We were not disappointed; our only regret was that we hadn't learned of it sooner. We suddenly felt a great desire to live in the beautiful red rock valley near the foot of the La Sal Mountains. We began making regular trips to Moab during our winter vacation; the weather was always clear and very temperate. On a midsummer vacation to Moab one year, we took a jet boat tour with Tex McClatchy down the Colorado River to the base of Dead Horse Point, a majestic cliff with a scenic overlook on top, some two thousand vertical feet above the river. Little did we suspect that, seven years in the future, I would become Tex's first full-time jet boat operator.

We bought a subscription to the Times Independent, Moab's weekly newspaper, and had it sent to the hardware store in Indianapolis. Sam Taylor, editor of the paper, told us at the time that when someone from out-of-state begins subscribing to the Moab paper, it's usually a good indication that he will some day become a resident of Moab.

64

I was hooked. I was a big fan of Moab and the surrounding area and didn't hesitate to tell everyone about it who would listen. I put together a slide show of the newly-established Canyonlands National Park. Arches National Monument had not yet achieved park status but would soon. It, too, was included in my slide presentation.

One hot, muggy day in August, a couple of guys walked into the hardware store and said they'd heard I wanted to sell the place. I said I had considered it and quoted them a figure, but it was more than they were willing to pay. They countered with a lower sum and said they'd give me time to think it over. They were going up to northern Indiana to look at another store which was for sale and would get in touch with me upon their return. When they came back, we dickered a little - very little - and they found themselves the proud owners of a successful, operating hardware store.

Jean asked what we were going to do next. I told her I planned to contact Tex McClatchy in Moab and see if he could use a jet boat operator that summer and, hopefully, subsequent summers. Tex was willing to try it and, lo and behold, within the next several months Tex and I made jet boat trips on the Colorado River one of the more popular activities for visitors to the Moab area.

The name "Colorado River" tends to evoke a mental picture of wild rapids roiling through primitive canyons. Although this is partly accurate, some stretches of the river are actually quite serene. It comes as a surprise to most visitors to Canyonlands that a 70-mile stretch of the river has no rapids at all. Another fallacy associated with the Colorado River is that it is always sluggish and mud-brown. For the most part, it is not a muddy river. Due to spring runoff, it has a high silt content which decreases later in the summer. By the middle of July, the river usually becomes quite clear. I have taken photographs in late summer in which the river is a clean, startling blue.

August is the month for localized desert thunderstorms. These brief storms make for some excellent photographs if one can just manage to be in the right place at the right time. Often, the sky turns a deep purple with frequent flashes of white and pink lightning, and time-exposure settings produce dramatic photographic results. September, too, is a lovely month for the camera buff, with the deep, dark greens of late summer. October brings brilliant autumn hues: in the valleys and canyons, massive cottonwood trees turn a rich gold; in the La Sal Mountains, the Gambel oak in the foothills is blood-red, and the quaking aspens vary from bright yellow to fiery orange. These warm, glowing colors contrast sharply with the violet-blue sky and its huge, fluffy clouds. The palette is made complete by the vivid red rocks and canyon walls.

Colorado River near Moab   *F.A. Barnes*

CHAPTER NINE

HOOSIER JET BOAT GUIDE
IN CANYON COUNTRY

I had never given much thought to committing my enthusiasm for canyon country to paper until I was approached by a friend who suggested I document my experiences as a guide.

To be a guide - a good guide - you must genuinely like people. And patience is essential. One must remember that we are all tourists somewhere at some time or another, and most of us have had the experience of asking what a local may consider to be some really stupid questions about the area we're visiting. It is a true skill to be able to answer these questions with grace and sincerity, letting one's expression reveal neither disbelief nor any hint of the impulse to burst into gales of laughter.

Most of my guiding experience has been on jet boats on the Green and Colorado Rivers and in four-wheel-drive vehicles bouncing through Canyonlands or Arches National Parks. I am not a pilot, but have also arranged and participated in some aerial guided tours. At the time of this writing, I have retired from the guide business, but still manage to cover a lot of backcountry.

Lin Ottinger, one of the first guides in canyon country, used Volkswagen microbuses to transport his passengers. These versatile vehicles were very capable of handling most rough trails. In fact, Ottinger is still using many of the original buses he had when he started guiding in the early 1960s.

Tex McClatchy, the first jet boat tour operator on that stretch of the Colorado River, came up with the idea of combining his jet boat tour with a microbus tour. The boat would depart from the dock in Moab and rendezvous with the microbus at Lathrop Canyon, a beautiful spot some forty miles downriver. This made for a very unique and enjoyable all-day tour. The microbuses had 40hp engines but these had some problems getting out of Lathrop and we often had to ask people to get out and walk up the steep hill. So the 40hp engines were later replaced with 50hp units. The VW had no doors, so getting out created no real problem; the driver would prepare his passengers for the upcoming bailout, then yell, *"Jump!"* when he started to lose steam. Nobody really minded this, and I was kind of sad to see this tradition go by the wayside when we got more powerful engines in the buses.

In 1968, Tex obtained a mold for what was, at that time, a very high-tech jet boat. This boat would carry twelve passengers without a lot of extra

Float plane in the high-desert

engine rev, which was very desirable, as it would increase capacity while reducing noise and vibration considerably.

Ten people had signed on for an all-day tour to Lathrop Canyon. We had room for two more adults, so Tex called the Moab chief of police and asked if he and his wife would like to come down for a free ride. About thirty miles downstream from Moab is a beautiful little grotto that we used as a "lunchroom." It afforded welcome shade - always at a premium in the desert - and a good view of the same escarpment where the Dead Horse Point State Park viewpoint overlooks the river.

After eating, we continued to an area across the river from Lathrop Canyon, which was our turn-around point, to view some ancient Anasazi Indian ruins, petroglyphs and pictographs. Upon our return to the boat, everyone was thirsty and we passed the water jugs around while I checked the engine oil. When all the passengers had boarded and we were ready to go, I turned the key and - nothing. Another turn of the key. Silence. Now, when you're captain of the ship, you're supposed to have all the answers. Everything is under control and there's nothing to worry about, right? Wrong. With no power, the boat was too big and heavy to paddle across the wide river, and I could easily see that the current, even moving at less than two miles an hour, was going to carry us beyond Lathrop Canyon and out into open water if we tried it.

The boat's canvas top happened to be secured with a very strong nylon rope. In one of my inimitable attacks of resourcefulness, I disconnected two sections of the rope and wrapped one section each around the two pulleys that would normally run an air conditioner on this 350-hp Pontiac engine. Since air conditioning is a dispensable luxury on a jet boat, I had both of these pulleys available. I handed the end of one rope to Ken, a husky 200-pounder, and the end of the other to a passenger almost as robust.

"Now, I'm going to count to three, and on three, both of you guys pull as hard as you can while I hit the starter button," I directed. Astonishingly, it worked! The engine started. The men shoved the bow out and we headed for home. I disconnected most of the instruments to save the battery on the way back and a few hours later we arrived at Tex's dock.

I was due to pick up four passengers and their canoes on a Friday morning at the confluence of the Green and Colorado Rivers. There had been some rain recently upriver in Colorado, but not enough to make the river rise, I thought. I left Thursday evening and decided to make camp about three miles above where the two rivers come together. Frank Murray, another of my boatman friends, had chosen to camp on the same sandbar, and it was nice to have someone to talk to. I laid out my sleeping bag about six feet from the river. Frank was an old hand at this sandbar-camping and I should have noticed that he had put his bag about twenty feet from the river. Before long, I was sound asleep. I was so weary that I didn't even take time to look for falling stars, as I usually did.

The next thing I knew, I woke up to a squishy sensation all over my body. It took a minute for my sleep-fogged brain to realize that the river had crept up to share my sleeping bag! Luckily, I'd removed my clothing and shoes and had left these articles out of its watery clutches.

On one trip down to the Confluence, I was to bring a load of canoes out in one of Tex's 24-foot jet boats. As I rounded a bend in the river, I saw a young man and a girl sitting on the north bank. I was a bit lonesome as I hadn't seen anyone all day, so I stopped to chat and make sure they weren't having any trouble. They had a canoe stashed in the bushes and planned to begin the strenuous paddle upstream the following day. I got the feeling they were pretty tired and weren't exactly looking forward to it. I was getting hungry and thought that just maybe the gal might not object to fixing an evening meal. I said, *"I've gotta go to the confluence for one more load of canoes. Do you want to ride down and camp with me and I'll take you back to Moab in the morning?"* They were all for it, so I loaded their canoe and gear in the jet boat and headed for the junction of the Green and Colorado rivers.

The girl fixed dinner and breakfast, too, and we all were revived enough to be almost enthusiastic about the return trip. We started out as the sun was just breaking over the lower canyon walls. That old Berkeley jet was pulling quite a load and I had a tough time "reading" the river because I couldn't see very well over the canoes and gear heaped up on the boat. We were getting close to the foot of Dead Horse Point, where the river is quite wide and sluggish, when it happened. I didn't even see the sandbar until we smacked into that sucker at a good clip! Every canoe on board went flying forward into the river. The young man almost went in along with the canoes but made a desperate grab for the bow lashing and hung on. The girl had been sitting beside me, so she was only thrown forward as far as the first seat.

After spending a considerable amount of time recovering all the canoes and gear which had scattered from here to breakfast, we tried to rock the boat off of the sandbar. It wouldn't budge. At this point, my passengers were getting a little worried. As I have mentioned, this was back in the 1960s and Canyonlands was unheard of by most travelers. Knowing this, my companions considered it unlikely that help would just happen along any time soon. However, the boat I was using was scheduled to go out again that same day, along with three other jet boats. I assured them that the wait would not be too long. Just as I was beginning to doubt my own assurances, we heard the drone of a motor approaching. The young man cried, *"That sounds like an airplane!"* Sure enough, good ol' Tex glided in and landed on the river in his float-equipped Super Cub. Not entirely optimistic about the chances of our getting towed off the sandbar by an airplane but nonetheless willing to try, we tied the bow line to the rear of the airplane. Then Tex cranked up the 150hp Super Cub to about 2200 rpm. All three of us began working the boat back and forth across the sand and in about ten minutes we were free from the sandbar.

Although I fervently hoped that such an adventure would never be repeated, it was comforting to know that this method of rescue was feasible in an emergency!

Alvin the Goat had his winter home at Tex's headquarters on the river near Moab. In the summer, he resided in the grotto where we ate our lunch on the jet boat tours. One spring, I was about halfway into a jet boat tour with my load of passengers when suddenly we heard a roar overhead that drowned out even the sound of the boat engine. Tex, in his pontoon plane, zoomed by overhead and disappeared in the distance. The passengers were dumbfounded. Here we were, miles from anywhere, no sign of habitation, when suddenly an airplane goes by less than fifty feet overhead. But one fellow was really shaken. *"Wh-wh-what was that **animal** on the pontoon of that airplane?"* he stammered.

"Oh, that was Alvin. He enjoys riding on the pontoon with Tex!" Then I explained that Alvin was a goat who spent about eight months a year at our lunch grotto and told the passengers that they would be formally introduced later.

Alvin the goat

Alvin knew our schedule and would come galloping down to the riverbank where we docked. Most of the people recognized him as a pet and laughed at his antics. Once in a while, however, people would fall for the gag and think it was really a wild goat greeting them.

Until 1971, Jean and I returned to Indianapolis each autumn after the tour season ran down. Both our mothers were getting up in years and, ironically, both passed away at about the same time. Our son Bernie was on a holiday break from college, so he and I made a quick run out to Moab to start plans for our permanent move. We talked to Bob Norman, a home-owner in the same area, about some of the difficulties involved in building in Kayenta Heights. We located several beautiful potential home sites there and later called Jean to enthuse about what we'd seen. She flew out and we ended up buying ten acres of land in the Heights with unsurpassed views. We talked to Paul Voth, a general contractor, about building the house, and Bob said he would arrange to get a well dug and an access road bulldozed. We left matters in those very capable hands and returned to Indiana to finish making arrangements for the move.

In February, I just had to see how things were progressing and decided to drive our Volkswagen bug out to Utah. J. D. Rogers, a young man whom we had known for many years, wanted to ride "shotgun." I had just had the engine rebuilt on the bug and didn't want to drive it very fast for the first 500 miles, but we kept hearing some ominous reports about the weather in Kansas and wanted to get through that state as quickly as possible. As is often the case in the midwest, the wind comes from the east prior to a big storm from the west. I thought it might be easier on the bug to take advan-tage of the tailwind. We got 'er up to about 70 mph with that tailwind pushing us and kept switching radio stations to get an update on the weather coming from the west. The wind started changing as we neared Kansas City, Missouri. By the time we got to the outskirts, it was snowing lightly. We topped off the gas tank, grabbed a quick sandwich and crossed into Kansas. The turnpike was still open, but we were told that the Interstate was closed west of Topeka and that U.S. 40 westbound would be closed within the next hour.

We got back on the Interstate and I put my foot in it, intending to go as far as possible before either the weather or road closure stopped us. The wind seemed to have subsided considerably, so we increased our speed a little. Despite the medium snow that was falling, we could run about 50 mph without any real problems. Or so we thought. I suddenly realized that I was having trouble steering the bug.

"Hey, J.D., I think our wheels are nearly frozen in a straight line!"

We stopped the car and got out to look. Sure enough, not only were the wheels encased in ice, but there was solid ice packed up in the wheel wells. It took about five minutes of kicking the front fenders so I could steer the VW. Things seemed to improve, but within another four or five miles the snow on the road was so deep that eight or ten cars had come to a complete stop on the Interstate. We didn't know exactly where we were, but found out the next morning that we were about five miles east of Manhattan. Fortunately, we had sleeping bags in the bug. Before crawling into them, however, we walked up the line of cars to see what the deal was. We learned that several men had taken off on foot to see if they could get some kind of emergency vehicle in to the car that was stuck in front of ours. The man driving that car had been headed to the hospital in Manhattan; his wife, who was in the car, was in the beginning stages of labor! I told her that we could probably get her through to the hospital in the VW, as we had been driving through fairly deep snow for quite a distance. She declined, thanking me and assuring everyone that she felt all right.

J.D. and I crawled into our sleeping bags and, surprisingly, actually got some sleep. The next thing we knew, it was almost daybreak. Within thirty minutes, we saw a road grader approaching. Because a VW's engine is in the rear, thus providing it with better traction, we were the first vehicle to make it out. I had one of my motorcycle racing helmets with me and decided to put it on for the trip into Manhattan just in case we should have an accident on the icy road. When we finally came roaring into a Manhattan gas station, the attendant looked at us like we were a couple of loonies! While filling the gas tank, he apprised us of road and weather conditions. The roads were closed west of Salina, Kansas. So we set out for Salina and made it there in time to get one of the few nicer motel rooms that were left. Things were not much better the following morning and the road wasn't to be opened until nine.

"J.D.," I said, *"it's gonna be a madhouse when this bunch takes off. Let's give them a good hour on the roads before we leave, because they'll all be in the ditches by then!"*

Sure enough, we left at ten and about 45 miles out of Salina, we came upon a line of cars backed up for several miles. They were in the ditches and all over the westbound lane at every which angle. We observed that the eastbound lane was completely empty, however, and it seemed a crying shame to let all that open road go to waste.

"J.D.," I postulated, "it's only about sixty or seventy feet across that median. Whaddya say we get a good run at it and plane across the snow to the eastbound lane? We might as well use it, since no one else is!"

I would estimate we were running about 50 mph when we left the westbound lane. We probably were still doing 30 mph when we hit the eastbound lane. We cruised along for quite a while, unimpeded. The line of incapacitated cars in the westbound lane was at least two miles long. When we were certain the westbound lane was clear, rather than remain any longer in the eastbound lane courting either disaster or a whopper of a ticket, I watched for a good place to return to the right side. We were old pros by now and had the opportunity to be a little more selective in our second crossover spot. We made it without a hitch.

Our next stop was Goodland, which is near the Colorado border. We obviously puzzled the station attendant by our presence since he knew the Interstate was closed west of Salina, but we chose not to explain and give ourselves away.

Once we were out of the lousy weather, the remainder of the trip was fairly uneventful and we coasted into Moab several hours later.

J.D. was anxious to see Canyonlands, especially the southern region, so we made plans to get an early morning start. On the way down, we saw a herd of what must have been about four or five thousand - not hundred, *thousand* - deer. Now, the reader may pooh-pooh this as being an exaggeration, however I later spoke to Rusty Musselman about the inordinately large herd and he said that he had seen it several times himself and agreed that my appraisal of the size was accurate. Later that day, J.D. and I drove down to Horse Canyon, the site of several spectacular arches. Among these are Fortress Arch, Castle Arch, Gothic Arch, Tower Arch, and Paul Bunyan's Potty. There is also an Anasazi pictograph panel in Horse Canyon known as the Thirteen Faces. For those unfamiliar with Anasazi rock art, a pictograph is a drawing made on a rock face using a medium such as paint or some other type of pigment. It is not chipped into the actual rock surface, as petroglyphs are. Pictographs are much less common in the southeastern Utah area than are petroglyphs. Lamentably, several years ago, three of the pictographs were erased when a huge flood swept through Horse Canyon.

74

Some of the Thirteen Faces

Since evening was drawing near, we headed east on the surfaced road that led back to U.S. 163 (now 191). We stopped and decided to camp at Indian Creek, near Newspaper Rock. J.D. had briefly seen this unusual concentration of petroglyphs on our way down, but now he could really look closely at the display of the ancients' rock art.

Our objective the following day was to drive down Butler Wash. We had heard of some Indian ruins along the east side of Comb Ridge that were supposed to be extremely well-preserved. We succeeded in finding them and spent a couple of hours poking around the site before heading back to Moab. We hung around town for a few days more, checking on progress on the house, but both J.D and I had to be back in Indianapolis, so we said our farewells and headed east.

CHAPTER TEN

LOCAL COLOR

For many years, the film industry has recognized Moab as an excellent area for shooting movies. Producer John Ford and actor John Wayne considered Monument Valley and Moab the perfect spots for filming their Westerns. The movie <u>Comancheros</u> was filmed in Moab in 1961. Jean and I liked to visit the site during location, where we frequently had an opportunity to chat with "The Duke." Much to my delight, I once got to take Ricardo Montalban on a river tour. Embarrassingly, when he stepped out of the boat onto the riverbank, the sandy ledge gave way and he wound up falling into the water, completely destroying his dignified reserve. Nearby Castle Valley has also become very popular with film crews in recent years, mostly as a location for filming television commercials and magazine ads. In the mid-1960s, Chevrolet advertised using a scene in which a new convertible was displayed on top of Castle Rock, a 1,500-foot-high pinnacle in Castle Valley. This went a long way toward establishing the popular trend of on-location commercials, particularly those needing western desert landscape. The opening scene in <u>Indiana Jones - The Last Crusade</u> was filmed in the Windows section of Arches National Park, about four miles north of Moab.

Castle Valley

Parts of <u>Thelma and Louise</u>, the 1990 Academy Award-winning film, were shot in the Moab area. Several months before the filming began, I suspected that a major production was being planned locally because several old convertibles were being brought in from out of town and were undergoing body work to make them all look alike. I assumed they were to be used as stunt equipment. I poked around some and found out that these cars would be used to film the final, dramatic scene in which the two title characters drive their old Mercury convertible off a cliff, in this case a 650-foot cliff above the Colorado River.

I got my video camera out and headed down the south bank of the Colorado on my 185 Suzuki to a spot opposite the place the film crew was to shoot the scene. I waited about an hour, during which time some friends of mine came up in their Jeep and joined me. We hid the vehicles where they were out of camera range and watched the film helicopter get into position for the big event. The convertible was rigged up on a windlass on a big steel cable hooked to the bumper hitch of a V-8 pickup truck. The truck powered up and roared off, triggering the windlass and propelling the convertible with its dummies off the cliff! I don't know whether the scene we got to watch was a "take" or not, but my friends and I certainly found it exciting!

I once provided guide services for a group of nine young Chinese women, none of whom spoke English. It was their first visit to the United States. Their driver was able to speak and understand some English, so he acted as interpreter. We were bound for the Island-in-the-Sky District of Canyonlands National Park, and planned several photo stops along the way. After leaving the highway, we made our first stop at the same place where I had watched the movie company filming the John Wayne picture I mentioned. Thinking it might be of interest to the group, I related this to the driver. Somehow, something changed in the translation, because suddenly I had nine little Chinese gals all over me, wanting to have their pictures taken with Fred Radcliffe, famous movie star and best friend to John Wayne! I can't rightly say that I did a whole lot to disabuse them of the notion that I was a celebrity - I mean, it isn't every day that a guy like me is the object of such adulation. I endured it, thankful that they didn't ask me for my autograph. I don't think I could've kept a straight face!

Tex used to have a tour shuttle bus that was fancied up to look like a paddlewheeler, patterned after his 90-foot sternwheel river boat, The Canyon King. I would drive this bus around town and pick up passengers for the jet boat tour. I had rounded up about fifteen people and was on my way to the dock. Among those on the shuttle were some folks from Germany. As we headed out of town, I saw a Hopi Indian friend of mine, Strongbow, crossing Main Street just ahead of us. *"Hey, Strongbow,"* I yelled. *"Come on over here and talk some Hopi to my tourist friends from Germany!"* I thought this might be an interesting experience for the foreigners, as Indian languages are very different from European tongues. They are quite guttural sounding and extremely difficult to learn.

Ol' Strongbow trotted over to the shuttle and smiled at my passengers. I was feeling smug, anticipating the look on the Germans' faces when they heard this authentic Indian rattle off something in his native Hopi. Well, I nearly fell off my seat when my Indian friend opened his mouth and out came fluent German! Then I remembered that he had served in the Army, although I hadn't known he'd been stationed in Germany. After a brief but animated conversation between Strongbow and the German passengers we proceeded with our tour, but I think my face was red all the way to the dock!

Despite its ominous-sounding name, Poison Spider Mesa is one of the most scenic spots in the country surrounding Moab. The turnoff to Poison Spider Mesa is located about six miles west on Utah 279, referred to by the locals as the Potash road. This mesa, with its stupendous views, is a favorite for mountain bikers, dirt bikers, and four-wheelers.

Former Moab newspaperman, Dick Wilson, first publicized the existence of Poison Spider Mesa in the early 1960s. On one of his forays on his Honda Trail 90, Dick accidentally dropped an expensive camera over the rim at one of the overlooks and it landed in the rocks some 600 feet below. He managed to recover the film and used the photographs to illustrate his Poison Spider Mesa story the next week in the Times Independent.

There is a series of fairly well-established trails over the mesa. Ber Knight, one of the most avid four-wheelers in Moab, and some friends of his developed the trails, including completing the loop all the way over to Little Valley. Fran Barnes, a longtime local, has mapped the main trails up on Poison Spider and I suggest that anyone coming into this country for the first time obtain one of these maps. Barnes, the owner of Canyon Country Publications, writes and publishes many books and maps which are extremely useful in exploring just about any part of southeastern Utah. These publications are widely available and are probably the most accurate guides to the backcountry in this area.

I believe that Mel Swanson and I were the first to make the north-to-south trip over the mesa via motorcycle. We had a couple of dirt bikes with 185cc and 250cc engines. I probably hold the world's record for the number of times across Poison Spider Mesa on a motorcycle - as of 1993, I have done it forty times!

One of our local tour operators, Jim Sarten, kept badgering me to take him up over the mesa sometime. Jim had lived around Moab for nearly thirty years, but he had never been up on Poison Spider. Finally, we took my four-wheel-drive vehicle up. He was completely enthralled with the place - that is, until we busted the radiator in the four-by-four. Now, the temperature up there was probably a good 100 degrees. Even in the desert, with its low humidity, that kind of heat can sap one's strength pretty quickly. Fortunately, we had a couple of gallons of water with us, which we lugged the five or six miles on foot back to the paved Potash road, where we caught a ride back into town.

The big problem at that point was how to get the four-wheel-drive back down off the mesa and into Moab. Rather than impose on friends, I went up the following day on my motorcycle to see what I could do about getting it out. I removed the beat-up fan, started the engine, turned the vehicle around, and drove up a short incline, keeping a close eye on the temperature gauge. Then I cut the engine and coasted several feet down the rocky incline. I repeated this process several times until I had covered a little over two miles and had just about run out of daylight. The following day I went up with a friend in his four-wheel-drive and he pulled me over the steep hills so I could coast down the other side. By the end of the second day, I had completed the 900-foot descent from the mesa to the river road with no apparent additional damage to the vehicle. If I were a drinker, Sarten would still be buying me beers for that one!

Some motorcycle buddies of mine from back in Indianapolis came out to Moab one summer with their dirt bikes. They were camping at the Slickrock Campground just north of Moab. I was scheduled to conduct a jet boat tour and so had to wait to bike with them until after I had completed my 80-mile round trip down to Lathrop Canyon. When I arrived at their campsite on my 185 Suzuki, the first thing they asked me was why I was wearing a leather jacket when the thermometer was reading well over 100 degrees. I explained that we would be riding over rock much of the time and leather is invaluable protection should one happen to take a slider down a hill. These guys were all excellent riders, so I was not too concerned about any of them falling.

Our destination was a fabulous viewpoint on the mesa overlooking Corona Arch. For many years, this was referred to on maps as "Little Rainbow Bridge," but it is really an arch, as it does not have and never has had a watercourse under it. Viewing the arch from high above entailed riding the motorcycles up several very steep slickrock foot trails. When I showed the fellows the course we had to take, they said almost in unison, *I'm not going to ride up that!* But after I demonstrated that it was easier than it looked, they all pulled the hill with no mishap. We crossed the mesa and rode down into Little Valley. We all managed to keep the bikes shiny side up, but I really showed those guys some rough terrain. When they returned to Indianapolis, they told all their riding partners, *"If Radcliffe ever shows up to take you on a motorcycle tour and is wearing those leathers, don't go with him!"*

Corona Arch from Poison Spider Mesa   F.A. Barnes

80

One morning, Jean and I were talking to our neighbors, Al and Loretta Kern, when the subject of the Book Cliffs arose. Al and Loretta had never ventured more than a couple of miles into that area, so I suggested we take a drive far up into the Books to the Ute Indian Reservation, the boundary of which lies some twelve miles north of Thompson, off Interstate 70. We hurriedly threw together some provisions and even included our sleeping bags in case we had to stay overnight for any reason.

About four miles north of Thompson is the old town of Sego, a coal-mining town that at one time was home to over 1,000 inhabitants. Sego supplied coal for the locomotives which traveled the nearby east-west railroad. With the advent of diesel engines, however, the coal-burning locomotives became a thing of the past and, along with them, small coal-producing towns like Sego.

Portions of the two main buildings in Sego still stand. The general merchandise store, built mostly of stone, is largely intact, with only the roof and windows missing. The boarding house remains distinguishable, but is in much worse shape than the general store. Several other smaller stone structures also remain, but have been damaged extensively by vandals.

General store, Sego   F.A. Barnes

Unless there has been a recent storm, two-wheel-drive vehicles can follow the road for about nine miles past Sego, or to about 8,500 feet in elevation. Beyond this lies the Ute Indian Reservation. In the early 1970s, there was no locked gate across the road preventing access to the reservation. Licenses could be purchased in Thompson to allow visitors to fish in beautiful Weaver Lake. At the time of this writing, though, it is no longer possible for outsiders to proceed past the gate and onto reservation land.

After entering the restricted area, the road drops down several hundred feet into Steer Gulch, climbs again to about 9,000 feet, then forks at Chandler Creek. The easterly route leads to Pioche Spring, Weaver Lake, and beyond. The other trail can be followed all the way to Vernal, Utah.

We were descending the Weaver Lake trail when Al happened to spot something shiny in the road. We stopped and he got out and went over to it. It was a piece of chert, a hard, whitish, glassy stone frequently used by ancient Indians to make arrowheads and spearheads. He dug it out of the road with his hands, cutting one of his fingers in the process. Sure enough, it was an arrowhead!

After leaving Weaver Lake, we climbed another 500 feet or so. The scenery was breathtakingly beautiful, and it was a perfect place to eat lunch. We ate, then decided to backtrack to Chandler Creek. There, we descended Chandler Canyon to the Green River and drove a spur trail downriver for about ten miles to Florence Creek. When we arrived at Florence Creek, we met river rafter Bill George, who informed us that, officially, only Indian vehicles or vehicles with permits were allowed on the stretch of trail we had just covered, but he said the Indians didn't usually enforce that restriction. Just then, a couple of Indians drove by and looked, but said nothing to us.

Old ranch at Florence Creek   J.A. Barnes

82

The old ranch at Florence Creek used to be operated by the Mc-Pherson family until it was sold to the Ute Indian tribe in 1939. The Indians built a beautiful pink stucco motel with about ten units which was intended to cater to hunters and fishermen. For some reason, probably the remoteness of the area, the motel never went into operation.

We returned the way we came in, climbing out of the river gorge via Chandler Canyon, then took the trail which leads to Vernal. On the way, Jean spotted something that we never had any clue existed. There, on a rock face near the road, was a petroglyph depicting the wreck of a narrow-gauge train which, we later discovered, had occurred in 1905 near the town of Mack, Colorado!

It was getting close to sundown when we arrived at a well-traveled road which eventually led to the modern town of Vernal. After stopping for about an hour at a restaurant and a gas station, we headed back to Moab. We got home about 2:00 in the morning, exhausted but feeling like truly great adventurers.

A few of the many prehistoric petroglyphs in Sego Canyon   F.A. Barnes

CHAPTER ELEVEN

GAGS AND GLITCHES

My son Bernie was probably about fifteen years old. He had been dying to accompany me on one of the river trips so that he could take his sleeping bag, some food and water, and camp out overnight at Lathrop Canyon. The timing was perfect. I had booked people several days in advance, so I could drop him off at Lathrop and pick him up the following day.

Bernie and I decided that it might be fun to play a little joke on our guests so he hid all his camping gear in the bow of the jet boat. As the guests came aboard at Tex's dock, I introduced Bernie to each of them. Nothing was said about his plans to disembark and camp at Lathrop. About 2:00 that afternoon, we pulled in to our landing spot and Bernie secured the boat to a tamarisk tree. After all our guests had gone down the foot trail, Bernie unloaded his camping gear, stashed it in the bushes, then disappeared. My visitors and I took the leisurely hike to the nearby ruins and petroglyphs, then back, a walk of about thirty or forty minutes. We milled around for a little while, chatting and quenching our thirst before boarding the boat again. As I was untying the rope from the tamarisk, one of the passengers asked where Bernie was.

*"I don't know, but he's **always** late and he knows perfectly well what time this boat leaves. Well, I'm going to teach him a lesson he won't forget! I'll be back to pick him up tomorrow!"*

As I shoved the boat off the bank and fired up the engine, Bernie burst from the bushes, hollering, *"Hey Dad! Wait for me!"*

"Nope, I'm fed up with your always being late. You're gonna learn better, one way or the other! Adios! I'll see you tomorrow!"

My guests were shocked to the core at the callousness I had just displayed toward my own offspring. I could see them whispering back and forth and looking askance at me. They just knew they were trapped in the wilderness with some heartless killer who would put his own son out to brave the elements, wild animals, and certain starvation. I let 'em think just that for about two miles before I had to shut down the engines and give in to a fit of laughter. Then they were totally convinced I was a lunatic until I explained that Bernie was voluntarily being left behind. Finally, they all loosened up and I think some of them even appreciated the joke.

I pulled a similar stunt in which my co-conspirator was a young mother with two boys. She wanted to camp at Lathrop for a week and made arrangements with me to bring her food and water in exchange for helping me play a joke on my passengers. On the way to Lathrop, I bragged to my tour group that I had two wives but that I kept one of the wives, along with two sons, a secret from the other one. As we pulled into shore, she came running down the trail, exclaiming, *"There you are! We missed you yesterday!"*

My passengers were aghast, albeit somewhat excited about encountering a real, live polygamist. I hope I didn't disappoint them too much when I explained that it was all just a gag!

Bernie takes the helm

Bernie had just acquired his jet boat operator's license and was taking his first group of passengers downriver. Normally, the full-day tour to Lathrop Canyon and back wrapped up at about 4:30 p.m. This particular day was a little different as we had scheduled a special tour to the confluence of the Green and Colorado Rivers, where two of the passengers would transfer over to a raft and continue downriver through Cataract Canyon. The remaining six passengers would come back upriver with Bernie.

The plan proceeded according to schedule. The two rafters were dropped off, and Bernie made good time getting back up to Lathrop, where he decided to make a 15-minute rest stop. While the passengers were stretching their legs, Bernie checked the engine and fluid levels just to be on the safe side.

"Okay, it's getting late, folks, and we have 42 miles to go, so let's get aboard," Bernie called. "This'll probably be a nonstop run!"

Normally, the pilot would start the engine and back off the bank into the river, but Bernie didn't this time, as he knew there was a problem with the reverse mechanism and he didn't want to aggravate it. He enlisted the aid of one of the huskier men and they pushed the boat off the sand. As soon as Bernie tried to put the boat into forward gear, though, he detected a strange sound issuing from the engine compartment. He made a split-second decision: he grabbed the bowline, jumped into the river and pulled the boat back to shore. Had he not done this, the boat would have floated downriver and out of range of any kind of rescue attempts made by air or land. It soon became apparent that Bernie's caution was not undue, as further investigation revealed that the timing chain was fouled up and only a skilled, equipped mechanic would be able to fix it.

When Bernie and his guests didn't appear at the dock in Moab at the appointed return time, Tex and I got a little worried. I was wondering how Bernie was dealing with the idea of a potential overnighter with six passengers - and on his first solo trip, no less! We gathered up some sleeping bags and provisions and took off for the airport where Tex's plane was parked. Once aloft, we headed toward the Colorado River and followed it downstream. The sun set long before we passed Dead Horse Point, but as we came around the bend and saw the boat moored at Lathrop, our spirits rose. With Tex flying as low as caution allowed, I leaned out the window and we began making our "bomb run," that is, dropping sleeping bags and provisions to the cheering castaways.

Since we were not in Tex's pontoon plane, we couldn't land on the water to ascertain the nature of the mechanical problem that Bernie was obviously having. Therefore, when we arrived back at Tex's place, I hopped in one of his VW buses and drove the fifty-plus miles out to Lathrop Canyon. Winding down the Shafer Trail, a steep and unimproved series of switchbacks, in the dark was a first (and I hope last) for me! I arrived at my destination at midnight to find everyone safe, although I nearly ran over one lady who had thrown her sleeping bag down in the middle of the road! Everyone was happy to see me, but none of them were too enthusiastic about getting out of their warm bags, climbing into the VW, and making the return trip to Moab right that minute. So I joined the group for the rest of the night. The next morning, we bussed back up the Shafer Trail and rolled into Moab in time for a hearty breakfast.

Shafer Trail switchbacks   F.A. Barnes

I remember playing a joke on the group of tourists that Bernie took out on one occasion. He was scheduled to drive one of the Volkswagen microbuses and its load of sightseers down to Lathrop Canyon. There, I would meet them in the jet boat and we would swap passengers for the respective return trips. My load of passengers had been clued in on the gag. Bernie deliberately arrived at the rendezvous a little early to play his part in the spoof. Our watches were synchronized to the second. I was just slowing down and coming off plane as I rounded the last bend before Lathrop. Bernie was there, waiting.

I had a pair of prescription glasses which I'd had specially made for summer use on the river. I have mentioned that I am abysmally nearsighted without glasses. These special glasses were quite dark and it was impossible to see my eyes behind them. I also had a cane that my father had used in his later years, when he fell ill with lung cancer and had difficulty getting about. Anyway, I had painted this cane white to go along with the very dark glasses. (I think the reader may have already guessed where I'm going with this.) Bernie had his group right down on the water's edge and I could see that they were excitedly anticipating the second half of their tour. They were hot and dusty and eager to hop on a jet boat and zoom down the Colorado. They could hardly wait to get aboard! So I pulled in real close to shore, got the white cane out and started thrashing the water.

"*Am I close to shore, Bernie?*" I asked hopefully.

"*Yeah, you're close, now turn to the right, Dad - now some to your left - that's it, straight in. Good show, Dad! I knew you could do it this time!*"

Oh, I'll never forget the looks on their faces! You can well imagine the confusion and consternation they must have experienced when they discovered that they would be making the return trip to Moab at top speed in a jet boat with a blind pilot who couldn't even find the shore by himself!

Tex McClatchy F.A. Barnes

88

Tex, as his name implies, is from Texas - Olney, Texas, to be specific. He attended college in Gunnison, Colorado and became a teacher. He taught in California, Colorado and Utah. One of his former California students, Jim Giambruno, came to Moab to work for Tex as a sort of handyman-cum-jack-of-all-trades.

Our lunch stop on an all-day jet boat tour was a little over thirty miles downriver and Jim was spending a couple of days down there removing bushes to expand our lunchroom. Jim knew our schedule, so just before we rounded the bend with a load of gullible tourists, he walked upstream a half mile, got into the water and waited for the boat to come. We rounded the bend and acted surprised as we pulled alongside Jim. *"What in the world are you doing out here in the middle of the river, mister?"* I asked.

"Oh, I'm swimming down to where the Green and Colorado come together," he replied. We had already informed our passengers that the confluence of the two rivers was some 30 miles more downriver! We then pretended to take pity on this exhausted but ambitious swimmer and invited him to come into our grotto and have lunch with us, which he did. Naturally, the tourists were all agape until we let them in on the joke.

CHAPTER TWELVE

THE UNFORTUNATE ONES

On one jet boat trip, I saw a standard highway vehicle being driven along the top of the ridge above the river and commented to my guests that the driver was either crazy or a local who was very familiar with the terrain. One simply does not go driving the family grocery-getter up on top of cliffs like that. I gave it no more thought until a few days later, when I heard a news blurb on the local radio: *"A man who was staying in the Bowen Motel has been missing for four days. When he came in to the motel, he announced that he was going to surprise his son at the end of a seven-day raft trip."* I mentioned to Jean that this fellow just may be the one I saw driving along the cliffs that day.

I decided that I needed some more flat rock for a wall I was building, so I thought I'd take the Scout and trailer and head down Cane Creek toward the area where I'd seen the sedan. It was our typical, blazing hot summer day when I started up Hurrah Pass. Although it was only about 10:00 in the morning, it was already in the 90s and would likely get up to 105 degrees, a pretty common midsummer temperature.

Normally, I would have enjoyed the trip, but that day I had a premonition that what I would find at the end of the line was not going to be pleasant. A lot of things went through my mind. It's amazing how many people will venture out into the burning, waterless desert, ill-prepared. This canyon country is so unforgiving; all it takes is an engine failure, or a sprained ankle, or a little navigational problem, and somebody may never come back alive. Then again, I thought, maybe this guy had provisions and knew what he was doing and I'd come upon him sitting on a rock at the end of the trail having a nice glass of iced tea! But I was unconvinced.

In those days, the rough road up Hurrah Pass was not traveled by very many people, and fewer still ever went down the other side. I had seen a number of tire tracks before the summit, but very few as I started to descend the back side of the Pass. Directly across the river from Tangren's Ranch, I saw three or four fairly new tracks, one wider and more recent than the others. About two miles beyond the ranch I saw a sand trail branching off to the left which had obviously been unused for some time - except there were fresh tire tracks on it. There was only one set of tracks going in - and none coming out. I knew then, without a doubt, that it was all over for someone. If he had gone down this road three or four days ago and hadn't come out, the elements had probably got the best of him.

I headed along the same trail, which led to several old uranium mines which were worked back in the early 1950's. Looking up, I saw a glint of metal on the benchlands ahead. After driving about 300 feet, I could tell that it was a passenger car. The driver had apparently driven right over a small seep, or tiny spring which, had he seen it, would have provided enough water to sustain him. At this point, I knew the driver of the sedan was dead, because I could smell him. I hesitated, but continued until the stench nearly overcame me. I determined that the wind was coming from the west, so I circled around and got upwind of the body. The 1967 Chrysler was on a steep incline and its rear wheels were buried in the loose rock. The man lay on his back, head uphill, feet downhill, with his shirt open. His right arm was over his chest. All the car doors and windows were open, indicating that he had sat inside to escape the sun.

It looked like the vehicle had become stuck and the driver had tried to dig it out, overexerting himself and succumbing to heat exhaustion. I would guess that he had probably died shortly after getting stuck and had been dead for quite some time. If only he had kept his head, found the seep and quenched his thirst, and sought shade, or perhaps slowly attempted to work his way down to the river, he might still be alive. As it was, I felt very sorry for the son he had planned to "surprise" by showing up at the end of his river trip.

I was just returning from my morning jet boat tour when I spotted a life jacket floating down the river. Before docking with my tourists, I cut the engine back and circled around to the orange jacket. We can always use spare life jackets on our river trips. I reached out to grab it and - oops! - there was a body attached to it. Since I was not anticipating lifting a heavy weight when I grabbed the thing, the occupied life jacket slipped from my grasp and floated rapidly downriver with the current. I hurriedly swung the boat around and made a successful second pass, snagging the life jacket and its lifeless contents.

It turned out that this young man who, coincidentally, was from Indianapolis, had drowned about sixteen hours earlier in the Westwater Canyon rapids south of Cisco, Utah. Westwater is a wild stretch of white water, popular with experienced rafters. In the spring, the water is still quite cold and is rushing at several thousand cubic feet per second. The

91

walls in most of the canyon are steep and slick, and it is nearly impossible to climb out, even if one is able to navigate the rushing waters successfully and reach the river bank.

It is always wise to accord proper respect to the Colorado River, regardless of how harmless it may seem to be. Even when the surface appears slow-moving, there are roiling undercurrents which can pull even the strongest swimmer under and sweep him away. If, by some unfortunate circumstance, an unlucky rafter should fall overboard in the white water, chances of survival are even slimmer.

It was early April, before the jet boat season had officially begun. I was on my regular daily run which departed the Moab bridge at 8:00 each morning and returned at noon. Not often did I have passengers from the Far East, but on this particular day a United States emissary to China and his family accompanied me on the trip. He was on furlough and they had come back to the United States to spend some time. We were on the return leg of the tour and approaching Gold Bar Arch. I glanced to the side and caught a glimpse of what I immediately identified as a "floater," or body.

I decided that an unpleasant sight like that would probably upset my passengers, not to mention the idea of actually retrieving the body and taking it ashore, so I just kept my mouth shut and motored on in to the dock. After delivering the family to their motel, I went to the Sheriff's office and reported what I had seen. I knew about how fast the current was moving and was able to estimate the body's rate of travel downriver. The Sheriff and I trailered my boat, drove out to the dock, launched, and headed in the direction I had last seen the body. We had timed it well and only had to go about a mile upstream before we encountered it. Since the body was in an advanced state of deterioration, we wrapped a rope around it and slowly towed it back to the dock. Upon investigation, we learned that the deceased had been a duck hunter who had drowned in Grand Junction, Colorado, four months earlier.

Bernie had been on a search-and-rescue about ten miles up the Colorado River from Moab. A little girl had been swept into the river at the Big Bend area and, after a week, when it became evident that a rescue was

92

not to be accomplished, the search was called off.

Several days later, Bernie had a load of passengers on his full-day, 80-mile jet boat run. He wove his way through the many sand bars that test a pilot's skill. It had been a long day and, despite the surrounding beauty, a few of the guests began to nod off. Bernie was his ever-vigilant self, as a jet boat pilot must be if he wishes to remain one for long. That is how he spotted something out there in the river that struck him as odd. He couldn't exactly put his finger on it, but something was not as it should be. As he got closer, he saw a floating object and concluded that it was a body.

His was a rather touchy situation. There were children on board and Bernie had no desire to subject them to a potential trauma. Rather than stop immediately, he continued on a short distance. He then pulled the boat in under some tamarisk and whispered to a couple of the men what he thought he had seen. The problem was discussed in hushed tones by the adults aboard and it was decided that a shield would be erected on the shore to block the children's view while the men retrieved the body.

The retrieval was accomplished and the body was wrapped in a tarp and put into the boat, out of sight of the children. Naturally, this put a damper on an otherwise enjoyable day on the Colorado River.

F.A. Barnes

CHAPTER THIRTEEN

MORE DESERT ADVENTURES

Gordon Sherley and I had met on a jet boat tour back in the early 1970s. A jet airplane pilot hailing from Calgary, Alberta, Gordon was enthralled by the red rocks and endless canyons in southeastern Utah. Somehow, our conversation got around to motorcycles. Gordon had brought a 250cc Honda with him and I mentioned I had ridden motorcycles since 1937.

"If I were to come here with my dirt bike this fall, could you introduce me to some of this canyon country I keep hearing so much about?" he asked. I assured him that I could and suggested that I take him out for a spin while he was in Moab. For a novice rider, he held his own quite well.

I never really expected to hear from Gordon again but, sure enough, in late September he called and said he would be coming to Moab the following month. Ours turned out to be a wonderful friendship. He visited many times after that, in every season, and became an excellent backcountry rider.

One autumn morning, Gordon, Jean and I set out in the International to a dirt road about two miles past the Dewey Bridge on Utah 128. We unloaded both motorcycles and Gordon and I said goodbye to Jean. We headed northwest toward Thompson, which is just off Interstate 70. A good stretch of this road ran through the Mancos Shale formation, a type of terrain which is not the most desirable for riding, as it is very loose and tends to slide. After a time I sort of lost my sense of direction. The rough trail we were on sure didn't give us any clue and there were no familiar landmarks. Finally we came up over a rise and in the distance we saw traffic moving along Interstate 70. I didn't want to ride either west or east to get across the highway, because it was easy to go too far in either direction and become disoriented. Then we spotted a wash that had swinging gates we could open up and go underneath a small overpass. I got through both gates without any problems, but Gordon forgot that he had a pack on his back and when he tried to go through, he ended up wedged under the little bridge, stuck fast!

"Hey, Fred, give me a hand, I'm stuck under here!" he yelled. *"Sure enough, buddy, but first I wanna get your picture all scrunched up under that bridge!"* He got even with me the next day when we were in Cane Creek Canyon. I had managed to get myself rimrocked and was trying to lower my bike off a big boulder without scratching it. *"Hey, Gord!"* I yelled, *"give me a hand lowering this bike!"* Naturally, he had to take a picture of me practically giving myself a hernia - and took his darn time about it, too.

Harry Beach, of Hartford, Connecticut, first came to Moab in 1950. Traveling alone to California in his Swift airplane, he was intrigued by the maze of canyons he saw from the air and could not resist landing at the old Grand County airport south of Moab. George Fisher, who lived nearby, loaned Harry his Packard to drive into town. George was also from Connecticut, which was a real coincidence, as there were very few people in those parts at all back then. The uranium boom had not hit, and Moab was just a sleepy little mecca in the desert. Even then, Harry fell in love with Moab and always scheduled his trips west to enable him to spend some time in the little community.

In the summer of 1966, Harry brought his daughter to Moab. They had rented a VW Bug and were traveling around, introducing Lucy to canyon country. I was working for Tex and had the good fortune to meet Harry on one of my tours. I'm proud to say that our friendship developed quickly and we've remained friends for more than 25 years. I spent many hours in Harry's Swift, and later his new blue-and-white Mooney, flying over beautiful southeastern Utah.

As any canyon country devotee will acknowledge, there are many strange and awesome rock formations tucked away in remote corners of southeastern Utah. While we were flying with Harry one morning, Jean spotted an arch that neither of us had ever seen or heard of before. The next day, the three of us set out to satisfy our curiosity. We took a four-wheel-drive out in what we figured was the general direction of the arch, but were stopped short at a big canyon we couldn't cross. Harry was due back at Pratt and Whitney, the motor works where he was employed, so we set aside any further attempts at that time to locate the elusive arch.

In early autumn we packed food, water and cameras and set out once again to find the arch. We succeeded only in becoming hopelessly lost for several hours. Later, Gordon Sherley, my friend from Canada, came over with his dirt bike in the back of his Ford Ranchero. I told him I had the perfect backcountry trip lined up and described our futile attempts to find the mystery arch. Gordon was all for it. We saw Milt Galbraith, another friend, that evening and he wanted in on the action, too. We topped off the fuel tanks on the bikes and loaded them up onto the vehicles. In about an hour, we were on the trail.

Routes in that area are seldom used and we had to break trail more often than not. As any avid dirt biker knows, the shortest distance between two points is not necessarily a straight line. Even though a westerly tack seemed the most logical, we still wasted most of the day on wrong turns, dead ends, and backtracks. To make matters worse, Milt lost his keys and we ended up burning an hour or so looking for them - unsuccessfully. I don't think we ever even got close to the arch.

Frustrated, we returned to town and dug out the topographic maps to use on the next day's search. This time, we decided to use Gord's dune-buggy. This sand rail job had soft, oversized rear tires, which enabled it to scamper over even the roughest terrain while still affording some degree of comfort to its passengers. We started where we had left off the day before. We went farther west and drove out onto several overlooks, but by late afternoon we had to admit we'd struck out again and dejectedly headed back to town. We decided to run a few trails on the way back just to cheer us up and wound up with a flat front tire for our efforts.

Gordon had had enough, so I needed to find another sucker as persistent as I was to help me locate that arch. I was bound and determined to demystify the doggone thing if it took me the rest of my days! I talked my brother-in-law, Joe Malston, into accompanying me on one more trek in pursuit of this arch whose existence I was actually beginning to doubt. This time I drove my International Scout. We parked it on a high ridge so it would be easy to locate when we returned. We hiked several miles, checking areas we had not covered before. But again it was fruitless, so we headed back to the Scout.

"Where's the Scout, Joe?" We had followed a wash for quite a ways and had overshot the ridge on which we had parked it. *"I don't know, Fred. Where the heck is the Scout?"* After fifteen or twenty minutes of this, we found our way back. I hate to admit it, but I had just about given up on even finding the Scout that day, much less the arch.

I knew my friend Fran Barnes had maps of most of the areas from the Book Cliffs to the Arizona border and was familiar with all of that territory, so I decided to check with him and see if he had any suggestions which might help me find the arch. Fran thrives on challenges such as this, so he dug his maps out and we pored over them. He had a pretty good idea as to where it might be just from my description of the area. He and his wife, Terby, went out the next day and located the missing arch on their first try! I'd never have believed it if I hadn't seen the pictures he took. As it turns out, I was less than half a mile away from the dumb thing the whole time!

I had been acquainted with Eric Rosshaupter of Munich, Germany,

Mineral Canyon Arch   F.A. Barnes

for several years and knew he was capable of all kinds of climbing. But when he wrote to me one winter and asked if I could take him down into Monument Basin the following July, I was hesitant and felt I should explain to him some hazards we might encounter during such an adventure. First of all, July is the hottest month of the year, with an average noontime temperature of 100 degrees or more. But he was insistent. The Totem Pole, a stone pinnacle which rises 200 feet from the floor of Monument Basin, had piqued his interest, in addition to numerous other monolithic oddities.

Several years earlier, Ken Aiken, the former Moab police chief, and his wife had made the same trek Eric wanted to make. They consumed all of their liquids more quickly than anticipated and nearly died before getting out. With this in mind, I called Kevin Cheri, the head ranger at the Island-in-the-Sky District of Canyonlands National Park, and asked whether there were any regulations against hiking down into Monument Basin. He told me that there were not, but asserted that only a fool would try it in mid-July. Naturally, he advised taking plenty of liquids if we insisted on going, and recommended we avoid moving about much during the middle of the day. Of course, I knew all this but wanted to tell Eric, the typical stubborn Teuton, just what the authorities thought of his harebrained idea. I was hoping it would dissuade him - but I should have known better.

Paul Brown, a longtime friend of mine from Indianapolis, came along as support from the rim. He had a trick leg and didn't think it wise to venture into the Basin himself, but wanted to come along anyway. Eric and I completed the tortuous descent into the Basin proper, hiked to the base of the Totem Pole and up numerous side canyons. By the time we were ready to begin our climb out, we had already consumed most of our liquids, and the thirst resulting from rationing what remained began to take its toll on us. We did manage the climb but were on the point of collapse by the time we reached the vehicle. Despite the difficulty, the trip was well worth it.

The next time I went down into the Basin was in late November. My main purpose for going this second time was to shoot some of the final footage for our Canyonlands National Park videotape. I couldn't have chosen a better time. It was much cooler and the angle of the sun was just perfect for photography. The only problem I encountered was some snow and ice build-up in secluded areas.

Dick Marriot of the Marriot Hotel chain called me one day from

Maryland and asked if I would take some of his key personnel on a guided tour by motorcycle across Poison Spider Mesa. He said I had been referred by Dick Wilson, a friend and writer. I presumably performed this service satisfactorily, because I was hired for a second and a third time to act as guide to southeastern Utah's scenic wonderland. This third time, however, all my daredevil antics caught up with me.

I had just celebrated my 61st birthday and felt as fit as ever. All my riding companions, including Dick, were excellent fellows and most of them were good dirt bike riders. Our warm-up session took us up old Highway 160, past Dead Man's Curve, then north to the Dead Horse Point State Park turn-off. I took the boys down a sand wash to get a feel for their level of riding expertise. A couple showed signs of being fairly new riders or never having ridden sand before. Sand riding requires a different approach. As a novice rider, when you get the feeling that you're going to fall, you tend to want to back off the throttle. The proper thing to do in sand is to increase the power and scoot back on the seat. Once you disabuse yourself of the notion that going faster is more dangerous, you can begin to relax and enjoy the ride.

One of the better riders on a 460cc bike started getting serious air on the "whoop-dee-doos," but I was able to stay right with him on my 185 Suzuki. All of the faster riders stopped when I motioned that we should wait for the slower riders bringing up the rear. They took a while to arrive and when they did, I told the faster riders to go on ahead and wait for me, with the slower ones, when they reached the slickrock area. I then led my little group on a shortcut, planning to arrive slightly ahead of the rest.

Then I blew it. I saw what I thought was a 4-foot drop-off. I shut the throttle down, then realized it was only a 2-foot drop. I came back on the throttle too late and the bike went end over end. I rode it, then it rode me, then we repeated the process. I felt excruciating pain everywhere, particularly in my lower right leg. When my mechanical dancing partner and I finally came to rest, I couldn't reach the kill switch and the bike lay on top of me, jerking around noisily, until one of the riders ran over and turned it off.

Dick said, *"We'd better get you an ambulance!"* I told him there was no way an ambulance could make it back in to where we were and asked him to just get the bike started for me so I could ride it out. They all protested loudly, but went ahead and started up the bike and sat me in the saddle. I rode through the two miles of rough, sandy hills without stopping, then the twenty-plus miles on the highway to the hospital.

I had four broken metatarsal bones, a broken leg, and two broken ribs. This was the first time I had broken any bones and, believe me, the boredom I endured the first two weeks of inactivity bothered me much more than the pain I suffered!

It was a mid-July afternoon when Bob Jones, owner of Moab's Tag-a-Long Tours, called. *"Fred, I know that you have a broken leg, but I see you driving and getting around town as though nothing were wrong. Is there any possibility that you could take three people from Holland on a Needles tour?"*

"Sure, I can drive in to Angel Arch and back out without any big problem. With this walking cast, I can probably even hike with them up to a good viewpoint."

"Oh, I forgot to tell you - these people expressed a desire to go over Elephant Hill. They've heard about it and have seen some pictures of it."

Elephant Hill   F.A. Barnes

I thought for a moment. I didn't feel I was up to making the trip over Elephant Hill and back. This trail is one of the roughest in southern Canyonlands. I asked Bob to find out if his guests would consider this plan: we would enter at Dugout Ranch, then climb to higher ground near Cathedral Butte, about 7,000 feet in elevation. We'd then descend into Beef Basin, go down Bobby's Hole, over S.O.B. hill, and wind up on the back side of Elephant Hill. That way I'd only have to make the Elephant Hill trip once. The Hollanders accepted the proposal and, like most visitors to this country, were awed by the fabulous scenery.

As we approached the back side of Elephant Hill, all three of my guests' faces went ashen. This was more than they had bargained for! I think they actually kept their eyes shut during most of the climb and didn't even so much as breathe until we were on the downward stretch!

Bull Valley is just south of the Needles District of Canyonlands National Park. The easiest way to get there is to follow Cottonwood Wash south from Dugout Ranch. About four miles below the ranch headquarters, the road crosses the wash and begins to climb. About seven miles beyond the gate, you pass beautiful Cathedral Butte, then down into Beef Basin, as I have already described, and south to Bull Valley. Many ancient Anasazi ruins still exist in this region.

Anasazi ruins in Beef Basin   F.A. Barnes

101

Harry, my good friend from Connecticut, accompanied Jean and me on a campout there. We arrived in the late afternoon and quickly set up camp, a simple undertaking since no tents were involved. Harry was off by himself, poking around in some ruins in a cave, and came back chattering excitedly about having found an odd-looking rock. We all hurried over to the place he'd been looking to check out his find. He had discovered a very large metate, a dished-out stone which the Anasazi Indians used as a base for grinding corn. A metate was used in conjunction with a mano, or smaller hand-held stone, to grind the multicolored corn into meal. Finding a metate is not particularly unusual unless it is one which has been used on both sides, as this one had. We were all enthusiastic about Harry's find, but since the dang thing weighed nearly thirty pounds, we left it there.

Three years later, in early November, Jean and I decided to go back to Bull Valley and explore some more. I really wanted to get that metate and was certain that it was still there. I had a little difficulty remembering where we had camped before, since so much time had elapsed since our last visit, and we wandered around for quite a while until I was able to get my bearings. By that time, the sun was setting so we decided to make camp and go the rest of the way to the metate site in the morning. I was pretty sure we were within half a mile of the place. We got the Coleman stove and lantern out and Jean whipped us up some grub. We had picked up some dead pinyon limbs along the trail that afternoon and built a small fire to sit by.

Jean had better hearing than I did. After a few minutes, she said, *"Did you hear that, Fred?"*

"Hear what?"

"I heard thunder way off in the distance! Maybe we ought to break camp and get out of here. These trails can get slippery, especially as we approach the Cathedral Butte area."

Well, I wasn't about to break camp and leave. We had come too far to back out and I wasn't going anywhere without that metate. Despite the faint rumble of thunder in the distance, we finally went to sleep. I wanted to camp out under the stars, but Jean was not too keen on sleeping outdoors, so we crawled into the Scout and were soon sawing logs. During the night, I heard raindrops falling on the roof of the Scout, but when we awoke, the rain had stopped and in its place were dark, lowering clouds. Jean woke up, took one look at the gloomy weather, and immediately went back to sleep. I was undaunted. I crawled out of the sleeping bag and began getting the gear together that I would need to pack out the huge metate. Water and matches are a must in the wild and remote backcountry. I seldom ever took my binoculars, but did this morning. My old military backpack would be very handy to carry the heavy metate back to the Scout. A few food items topped off the necessities.

Time had dulled my memory and it took much longer finding the site than I had anticipated. There was a dense fog which lay in the lower areas, obscuring the upper two-thirds of the 300-foot cliffs. It seemed to be closing in even more so and visibility was decreasing. After about half an hour of searching, I located the cave with the metate in it. It appeared that neither humans nor animals had been in the cave since my last visit three years earlier. After a few minutes' rest, I put the metate in the backpack and started for the Scout. Since I was carrying such a heavy rock, plus all of the provisions I had brought, I naturally tried to choose the easiest route back to the car. I had to deviate several times from the path I had taken originally. The fog had lowered considerably. I began to realize that none of my surroundings looked familiar. The landmarks I had noted on the way in were nowhere in sight. I started to get a little worried; not about myself, but about Jean back at camp.

After walking around in what I later discovered were counterclockwise circles for about an hour, I noticed that the fog was lifting a little. I took off the backpack, got my binoculars, and climbed up a cliff to see if I could recognize any of the terrain. I had gone about twenty feet up a pile of rocky rubble when I saw a huge boulder, nearly perfectly round, and decided to step up on to it. When I put my weight on a smaller rock just below it, that rock slid, dislodging the larger boulder above me. I leaped sideways and the big boulder went crashing down the slope. It took a few moments for me to gather my wits and realize how close I'd just come to being crushed. Upon reaching a higher vantage point, I looked through my binoculars and finally spotted a familiar area where two canyons converged. Relieved, I decided to take a break and eat a little something.

After eating, I headed for the car with renewed confidence. About ten minutes later I knew I should be approaching a trail on my left. Everything was working out just as I figured. There was the trail and - wait a minute! The trail was not on the left, as it was supposed to be - it was on the right! I was 180 degrees off course! But at least I was on the trail and could find my way back to the Scout. I'd just have to go in the opposite direction. In another thirty minutes, I staggered back into camp with my trophy. I didn't see Jean anywhere! Then I found her in the Scout, sound asleep. She had slept right through my entire four-hour ordeal!

I must relate this little anecdote, if only to salve my pride and to prove that other guides can get lost, too. Tex McClatchy managed to get lost right on the Colorado River where there are only two directions in which to go!

Tex was alternately running three boats on the river, one of which I was piloting much of the time. When a large group of thirty came over from Grand Junction wanting a river tour, Tex had to find a third pilot, as the group would fill all three boats and we only had two pilots at the time. An aviator friend of Tex's, Dean Wissell, was pressed into service as pilot number three and was assigned the smaller jet boat. Dean was to follow Tex closely and I was to alternate between taking point and bringing up the rear.

Shortly after leaving the dock and going around the first sweeping bend of the river, I noticed that Tex had stopped and was down fiddling around in the engine compartment of his boat. When he finally emerged, Tex didn't realize that his boat had drifted around and that the bow was now facing upstream. He restarted the engine, threw it into forward and headed back upstream! His new boat pilot Dean did as instructed and closely followed Tex, disappearing around the bend back toward the launch ramp. I could not for the life of me figure out what was going on so I just killed the engine and floated there for a few minutes, waiting. Pretty soon, Tex came back around the bend wearing a sheepish grin and trailing Dean along behind. He admitted, embarrassedly, that he hadn't realized he was going the wrong way until he saw the launch area up ahead. The steep cliffs surrounding the river in that particular stretch all look pretty much the same and Tex was in such a hurry to get the show on the road that he didn't pay much attention to the direction of the current!

CHAPTER FOURTEEN

A POTPOURRI OF ODDBALL HAPPENINGS

At my suggestion, some visitors from California took an air tour with my pilot friend, Keith McFall. Seeing Canyonlands from the air is quite a thrill and one every serious sightseer should experience. My friends enjoyed it immensely.

The following day, I picked up this same group for a trip in my Volkswagen Bug across the Sand Flats road up to the beautiful La Sal Mountains. They were still raving about the air tour they'd taken the day before. Keith, who knew the area like the back of his hand, had given them a thorough session and did not leave out many of the scenic wonders. They were impressed with his knowledge and ability.

One of the major attractions we planned to view on our day's land tour was the beautiful Ponderosa forest about thirteen miles up the Sand Flats road. We had traveled about eight miles when we came over a slight rise and saw, in the middle of the trail, an upside-down Cessna 152! A figure was sitting on the ground next to the airplane, obviously the pilot of the craft. When I saw the man move, I was greatly relieved that at least one occupant had survived. A rather muffled voice spoke, *"Boy, am I glad to see you, Fred!"*

F.A. Barnes

"Is that you, Keith?" I asked, more than a little surprised. Sure enough. The poor guy had been sitting there in the blazing hot sun for over two hours after crashing his plane. He had a nasty bump on his head where it had been struck by a flying oil can which had been loose in the plane, and the prettiest set of mashed lips I'd ever seen. He was a little woozy from the beating he'd taken, as well as from the subsequent exposure, and pretty happy to see us. Apparently, a fuel problem had developed with the Cessna - we later determined that the attendant had failed to put sufficient fuel in the two tanks when Keith had his plane serviced at the Grand Junction airport - and he had attempted to make an emergency landing on the Sand Flats road. Unfortunately, the landing gear had caught on a sand dune just a few feet from the road, flipping the plane upside down in the middle of the road!

We loaded Keith into the VW and headed for Allen Memorial Hospital in Moab. I had the bug cranked up and was sliding around the corners, anxious to get him there quickly. Holding on for dear life, Keith muttered through swollen lips, *"Slow this crazy thing down, Fred! I don't wanna live through a plane crash just to die in a Volkswagen!"*

Needless to say, my California friends were quite relieved that they had gone on their air tour the day **before** instead of on that day. The upshot of the whole episode was that Keith gave up flying for good.

In the summer of 1970, my daughter Elaine, her husband Jim, my son Bernie, and his fiancee Paula, joined Jean and me on a campout in the Needles section of Canyonlands National Park. In order to get to Devils Kitchen where we planned to camp, we had to make the arduous drive over Elephant Hill. At this time, Canyonlands had been a national park for only six years. It was unlikely that we would meet other campers in this remote and unpublicized area.

We picked a campsite under a large overhanging rock with space to lay our sleeping bags out of the wind. We couldn't help but ponder the remote possibility of the rock's breaking and falling down during the night, squashing us all like bugs. Of course, that would have been ridiculous; that rock had been there for thousands of years! Needless to say, the huge monolith stayed where it was and we awoke our normal three-dimensional selves the next morning. Ten or twelve years later, however, I happened to take a tour group to that same area and - you guessed it - there the giant rock lay, in pieces on the ground. I will never forget the chill that ran up my spine at the sight of it. Never assume anything.

The chances of actually seeing a huge rock like that fall are pretty remote. I saw a spectacular rockslide while I was taking a bus group through Arches National Park. A tour company from Edmonton, Alberta, Canada used to bring a bus into the Moab area about twice a year. They usually called on me to act as their guide through Canyonlands and Arches National Parks. We always left the Park Avenue viewpoint in Arches for an impressive conclusion to the tour. On this occasion, as the bus was approaching the Park Avenue parking area, I began my spiel.

"Visiting friends, we are nearing the end of the Arches National Park section of the tour. We hope you have enjoyed this spectacular wonderland here in southeastern Utah. This, our last stop, features the magnificent Park Avenue viewpoint. I strongly suggest you bring your cameras. If any of you wish to have photos taken of yourselves with the cliffs in the background, give me your cameras and I will shoot the pictures for you."

Several visitors took advantage of this offer. I was just composing about the fourth picture when the side of one of the cliffs about 500 feet away simply peeled off and slid to the ground! Before I even heard the rumble, I quickly hit the shutter button on the camera; I'm sure I got the rockslide in action with a guest in the foreground. I meant to get the guy's address so I could ask him for a copy of the photo, but it slipped my mind. I'll always wonder about that picture.

Landscape Arch   F.A. Barnes

Landscape Arch in Arches National Park is often referred to as the longest arch in the United States, but another massive arch that vies for that record is Kolob Arch in Zion National Park. Landscape Arch, however, is undoubtedly the thinnest rock span for its length. In September of 1991, a huge piece of Landscape Arch broke off, rendering it even thinner and more fragile than before. Fortunately, no one was beneath the arch at the time, but one European visitor, standing a short distance away, was lucky enough to catch the startling event on video.

In 1970, a young man we knew from Indianapolis visited Moab. He had never been in southeastern Utah before and wanted to see some real honest-to-goodness Indian ruins. My son Bernie hadn't yet had the opportunity to see any good ruins either, so we decided to kill two birds with one stone. We arranged to visit the Baullie Flats area south of Moab, where there are several ruin sites. On the way to Baullie Flats is Comb Ridge, a beautiful and geologically fascinating area where many Anasazi ruins also are found. Both of these sites are only a couple of miles off of Utah 95. Several of the structures are still in good shape, although a few have been damaged by vandals.

My visiting friend was overwhelmed! Shortly after starting our tour of the ruins, I saw one that I had overlooked on my previous visits. It was

unlike the others in that it had an opening in the roof. At first we thought it to be a granary for storing corn, but that would not explain the additional entrance in the unusual location. Perhaps this was some type of ceremonial structure; I still have not discovered what its purpose may have been.

We were crawling along a precarious rim for a better look at some of these ruins, as there wasn't enough clearance for us to stand up. Bernie was in the lead. Suddenly, I heard him let out a yelp! He had rounded a sharp corner on his hands and knees, focusing close attention on the ground ahead of him, and had came face-to-face with an enormous golden eagle! Both equally startled, they eyeballed each other for one long moment before the eagle decided he didn't like what he saw and took flight!

SHOWALTER

Rather than return the same way, we worked our way on around the cliffs to the east side and found a passable way out. As we emerged, I noticed across the canyon yet more beautifully preserved ruins. As it turned out, I had to wait another year before going back to have a look at them. When I did, I found a series of numbers and letters pecked into the structural rock. I later did some research and discovered that these carvings were a type of identification mark used by early explorers from the Smithsonian Institution. The only other such marks I ever encountered, nearly twenty years later, were about three miles distant (as the crow flies) from these ruins.

One February, Gordon Sherley and I decided the weather was temperate enough that we could take our dirt bikes down to Davis Canyon in the Needles section of Canyonlands National Park. I had only been to Davis Canyon once before, about eight years earlier. Tex McClatchy had taken me down there one summer in his 40hp Volkswagen dune buggy and we had a delightful time romping around the dunes and slickrock, and exploring the many side canyons which branch off the main one.

It was a bit overcast when Gord and I arrived and began to unload the bikes. First, we headed up a tributary canyon but encountered a dead end, so we backtracked and took another side canyon. A little way up, we met a fellow in a four-wheel-drive. We chatted a while, then continued up the canyon, where we found and photographed an unusual Anasazi ruin built of pinyon logs. It was nearing noon, so we stopped at a shady spot and ate some of the grub we had brought along. After lunch, we headed back out to the main park road. We decided that, instead of going back exactly the way we had come, we'd follow a sand wash where we could make better time. To our surprise, we almost bogged down in quicksand and had to turn up the wick so that we could keep up enough speed to make it across the swampy stretches. We could see the paved road ahead and figured we had it made - that is, until we came to the barbed wire fence. Upon inspection, we determined that the way was impassable and we had to turn back and brave the quicksand again. This time, we were not quite gung-ho enough and the gooey stuff got us. The bikes became stuck repeatedly and it took us a long time to get out of that canyon. It's a good thing there were two of us there to help pull each other out!

You know, I seem to end up in the most interesting predicaments as a result of my determination never to take the same way out as I took in.

And I usually get some lucky stiff in the same boat with me! I don't suppose I'll ever learn, though. And so far, my reputation for these dilemmas hasn't become so widespread that people are wary of accompanying me into the backcountry!

Nearby Lavender Canyon was still virgin territory to us, so we spent the rest of the day exploring the many arches and Anasazi dwellings in that area. Surprisingly, Lavender Canyon was not so named because the rock bore any unusual purplish hues, as one would assume, but after a rancher who grazed his cattle in that region before it became a national park. His son, David Lavender, later became a well-known regional writer.

It was late in November and the tour businesses had long since shut down for the season. No more rafting down the Colorado, and even the largest tour company, Tag-a-Long Tours, had put all but one or two of their four-wheel-drive vehicles in mothballs. Their drivers, for the most part, were college students or seasonal employees who worked in ski resort towns in northern Utah or Colorado during the winter.

Bob Jones, the owner of Tag-a-Long, called and asked if I would take a jeep tour down to Angel Arch in southern Canyonlands. I had made several excursions to Angel Arch and always thoroughly enjoyed the trip - although I think I had gone there only once during the winter. I recalled that Salt Creek had been frozen solid, making passage easier than in the summer months; no more soft sand or countless fords of the creek. Bob said that there was only one fellow wanting to go and that he was so enthusiastic about the trip that he'd offered to pay double fare, although, truthfully, I'd have done it for nothing. So we headed south in Tag-a-Long's Toyota Land Cruiser.

No one was at the Park entrance station when we arrived, so we went ahead down the well-maintained blacktop road. We soon split off on a gravel road, which led to a four-wheel-drive trail. There was a little snow along the trail, but we had no problems. Salt Creek, despite some running water, was still easily passable. The sun was shining brightly, but I noticed some ominous dark clouds off to the south. I kept an eye on them but they didn't seem to be moving in, so I decided on a quick side trip up Horse Canyon to Paul Bunyan's Potty. Just about then, the dark clouds started moving, so we beat it back to Salt Wash. There now seemed to be more water in the wash than before, and I guessed that there was a hard rain

Paul Bunyans Potty   F.A. Barnes

falling in the higher country. As we approached Peek-a-Boo Arch, I suggested that my passenger walk through the arch and I'd meet him on the other
side. I directed his attention to some Indian "rock art" right near the opening
of the arch. With that, I started the engine and took off to get to the other
side before my passenger did. I was halfway around the rock fin when, all of
a sudden, the Toyota developed a sickeningly squashy feeling. I got out and
the cause was immediately apparent. I was up to my axles in quicksand!
Tag-a-Long provides, in addition to first aid kits, a handyman jack for each

vehicle. I got the jack out and scrounged around looking for flat rocks to put underneath it to give it a stable base. Pumping the jack frantically, I kept watching hopefully for any signs of progress. Instead of the vehicle beginning to rise out of the mire, the jack was simply disappearing into the quicksand. By now, my guest had become concerned and had walked back to the 4 x 4 to see what had happened. I had just about exhausted every conceivable plan to extricate the Toyota from its quagmire and had to explain to my patron at this point what our next move would be. I didn't want to alarm him, but felt compelled to point out how dark and close the clouds now were. He took that okay, so I proceeded to outline the plan.

"We're about five miles in from the entrance station and our only option is to walk back and get a ranger who can come in with a vehicle equipped with a winch," I explained. I asked if he felt up to walking that distance and he assured me that he could. We gathered up our extra clothing, a canteen, and some matches and started down the edge of the wash. The sky was really darkening, so I picked up the tempo a little. My companion seemed to be having a little trouble keeping up, so I suggested that he stay to the edge of the creek bed while I took off cross-country. I would get help and pick him up on the way back to the Toyota.

Tamarisk trees are not native to Canyonlands, but they have taken over in much of the country since their introduction to the west over 100 years ago. Originally a native African flora, tamarisk was imported in the early 1900s for use in stabilizing riverbanks and irrigation ditches. The tamarisk growth in this particular area was so thick in spots that I often had to get down on my hands and knees and crawl underneath it to get through.

I finally reached the jeep trail and made good time, as I was able to jog most of the way. Luckily, after having run and crawled for about four miles, I spotted a ranger in a jeep and flagged him down. He had a radio and contacted another ranger who had a vehicle with a winch. We struck out down the trail on the lookout for my guest who, in the meantime, had followed my trail and was out on the road, waiting for us.

With the winch, we soon had the Toyota out of the quicksand and were once more on our way. This time we stayed on the paved roads, just to be on the safe side!

I was sure that the trip had been a disappointment for my customer. I told him he was entitled to a full refund, but he declined! He said he'd felt like a real adventurer and that he didn't have any opportunity to really get in touch with the wilderness in the Pennsylvania city where he lived. He actually thanked me!

CHAPTER FIFTEEN

MECHANICAL MISHAPS

One summer, two young men, one from England and the other from France, called to reserve seats for a jet boat tour. I told them that the river had reached its lowest point - indeed, was lower than I had ever seen it - but that I would go check it again and call them if the water had risen enough to give a satisfactory tour. Shortly thereafter, a lady from Philadelphia also called wanting a trip and she, too, was placed on standby until a river check could be made. I wanted to be absolutely certain before giving the okay to tourists who might end up being disappointed, so I checked with the park headquarters and learned that a fairly heavy rain had fallen upriver in Grand Junction, Colorado, the night before. That was good news but, just to be sure, I made a final visual inspection of the river anyway. I was happy to see that it was up about eight inches from the previous day.

Now, I pretty much considered myself to be a first-class river runner who made few mistakes, but my "river check" would show that I really was not the bigshot I thought I was. I picked up my passengers at their motels, took them down to the loading dock, and shoved off. The trip began without a hitch. That extra eight inches made travel on the river a real pleasure. We motored through The Portal where the river divides the cliff wall and stopped at the petroglyphs on the north side of the river. Everything was going so well that I failed to observe that we had run out of deep water. About twenty miles downstream, I noticed that it appeared a bit shallower, but saw no reason to be concerned. The first indication that we had run ahead of the eight-inch rise was after we passed the upper petrified forest area.

I had shut the engine off and we were just floating on down the river when I felt the boat nudge onto a sandbar. I still wasn't too worried, but rather than start the engine and suck sand into the cooling system, I removed my shoes and jumped into the water. Beth, the lady from Philly, thought that looked like fun, so she joined me and, without our weight in it, the boat floated off the sandbar quite readily.

My original plan had called for a second stop on the way down at another petrified forest site, but I decided to continue on beyond Dead Horse Point and make that stop on the return back up the river. We had just come around the bend and my three visitors were oohing and aahing at beautiful Dead Horse Point. We made a stop at the spot which affords the best photographic composition of the point. Then we proceeded on down beyond the petrified log which sticks out of the left wall. I still didn't realize how shallow the river really was until I noticed that the petrified log was a good four feet above the water. I had seen it three feet above the water once or twice, but never four feet. Even with this observation, it still didn't dawn on me that the water was exceptionally low until I started the engine, got the boat up on plane, made the usual inside corner - and then - whammo! Right onto a sandbar at full speed.

Ordinarily, this would not have posed too much of a problem, but on this trip we lacked the manpower we needed to get the boat off the bar. The British lad was recuperating from an appendectomy and the French visitor seemed a bit shy on muscles. Beth was a real trooper and gave it her best shot, but we couldn't budge the boat even an inch. I outlined our options to the group: we could wait until the rising waters arrived so the boat would float off the sandbar, or we could climb the cliffs 500 feet up to a jeep trail and begin hiking back to Moab. The Frenchman was not convinced a jeep trail really existed in that wilderness. Nevertheless, the group agreed to give it a try. First, we had to wade through about 100 feet of very shallow water before arriving at the tamarisk jungle on the bank.

Finally, after navigating the thick shrubbery, we arrived at the base of a sheer cliff and proceeded to ascend via steep switchbacking curves. By the time we reached the first level area, my comrades were beginning to doubt that they had what it took to reach the top. It didn't help matters any when I suddenly realized that we were on the wrong ridge and were forced to descend about fifty feet and start anew!

I was carrying a two-gallon water jug and already my troops had put a good dent in it. At that point, I'm sure they were about ready to chuck me off the cliff, but we got under way again, and this time I was able to get them up the incline and on to much easier climbing. I could tell that their confidence in me was beginning to improve, thank heaven.

About midway up a series of switchbacks, we came upon a rocky overhanging ledge. The ledge gave us no more than about 36 inches vertical clearance and no more than 42 inches horizontal clearance. The two fellows didn't seem disturbed at this challenge, but Beth was frightened and said, *"Fred, I can't do it!"*

Now, by gosh, we weren't about to turn around and climb back down the cliff after having come this far. I said, *"Beth, you kneel on the inside of the slot and I'll get beside you on the outside, and we'll crawl through together."*

This calmed her down some, and we made it through the squeeze and reached the jeep trail within minutes. The trio of adventurers took several pictures of the Colorado River and the marooned jet boat, which looked like a matchbox toy from the rim.

After taking several more pulls from the jug, we started along the jeep trail. We had walked about three miles when a four-wheel-drive rounded the corner. In it was a very friendly family from South Dakota who had, providently, a CB radio. I called home on the radio and my wife asked my neighbor to come rescue us. Our Black Hills benefactors insisted on driving us to the point where we saw Jean and our neighbor coming up the dusty trail. Rather than being put out with me, my passengers thanked me for a wonderful, eventful trip that they would remember for years to come.

My next problem was that of retrieving the boat from the sandbar. After arriving in town, sweaty and exhausted from the day's exertions, I contacted Tex's office to tell them I was putting a canoe in the river at the Potash dock and planned to paddle down and bring the jet boat back somehow. Tex got the message and decided to fly down and give me a hand. He arrived at the sandbar just as I was paddling up in the canoe. The river had risen, as I knew it would, and the boat was almost free. In about five minutes, we had it floating and I was headed back up the river.

It was mid-September and the days were getting shorter. Tex had gone out of town and I was filling in for him, running the big twin-engine jet boat on the full-day tour. When everything was working like it was supposed to, this boat was a real beauty and a lot of fun to pilot. This 85-mile tour was my favorite, and September was the perfect month for it. The group on board was the kind a guide liked to be with. It was a good thing, too, because the group was going to be together a little longer than they anticipated when they came aboard.

My passengers had just shot up the last few frames of film remaining in their cameras as we passed below Dead Horse Point. The sun was getting low on the red cliffs, illuminating them beautifully. We were all reveling in the idyllic afternoon which was, as it turned out, too good to be true. The boat had two jet engines and two jet pumps, but had steerage through only one jet. Of course, since it was something we only had one of, it broke, leaving me unable to steer at all. I did manage, with the use of the engine and paddles, to coax the boat to a sandbar.

116

There was adequate water aboard and some food, so we weren't in dire straits - yet. I was scurrying around, delegating duties and trying to figure out a way to break the news gently that if anyone had an early morning appointment in town, they weren't going to keep it. I found most members of the group to be a little stubborn about gathering firewood for the night ahead when it was 90 degrees in the shade - which, incidentally, we had none of. I had never climbed out of this particular canyon before, but decided that I had better try to go get help.

I reached the top in less than half an hour. The sun was getting lower and, as I walked through the shadows, I thought I heard a car door slam. I ran up over a rise in the road and saw two men, neatly dressed, getting into their Chevrolet sedan. It appeared that luck was with me for a change, because it was highly unlikely that I would encounter help in that remote area at that time of the evening. Anyway, these guys drove me right to Tex's and dropped me off. As I expected, Tex had not yet returned from his trip.

Art Giese, an ace mechanic, had another of Tex's jet boats in his garage. I looked him up and explained my predicament. He agreed to finish work on the boat that night if I would give him a hand. We got after it and rolled the boat out of the garage a little after midnight. I towed it out to Tex's place, grabbed a few hours sleep, tossed some provisions into the boat and headed down the river. My group was happy to see me - I think there was a nagging idea in the backs of their minds that I might not show up!

A problem confronted me. The engine on the newly-rebuilt boat needed a few hours of break-in, but these people wanted to get the heck off the river - and quickly. With thirteen of us in a fully-loaded boat, I had to run the engine up to 3,000 rpm to get onto plane. After reaching a planing speed, I backed off a little and was able to get to the Potash dock without mishap. Eight of my passengers had parked their vehicles there and were able to disembark. This relieved some of the stress on the boat and we headed back to Tex's, expecting no further trouble. Silly, optimistic me! There was a lot of debris in the river which had washed down after a big storm in Colorado. I knew to keep a close watch for pesky little twigs that could get into the jet pump. This is a routine precaution and even if a twig or two gets in there, all I have to do is shut 'er down and clean out the pump. Sure enough, in a few minutes, I sucked a twig into the jet and I had to go inside the pump and clean it out. I replaced the intake cover, hit the starter and got no response. I lifted up the engine cover and saw that the starter mounts had broken off! This was a new one on me. I began to wonder what

I could possibly have done to deserve such terrible luck. What next?

I guess I was lucky to even have a paddle on board. We were also lucky to be within fifty feet of the Potash road. We weren't so lucky in that the fifty feet was comprised of thick, buggy tamarisk. We had little choice, however, so we paddled our way to shore and tied the boat to a small tamarisk tree. It was a good thing that I was accompanied by this jovial foursome because, despite all our problems, they remained in good spirits. The first seven or eight feet was flat, but then we had to climb vertically for about twelve feet to get onto the road. One of the ladies was in the lead. She had about three more feet to go to reach the berm of the road. Being terribly exhausted, she suddenly lost her balance and toppled backward onto her husband! This, quite understandably, put him off balance and he windmilled, falling backward onto the other lady who, in turn, went arse over teacup and flattened her husband at the bottom of the heap. Fortunately, no one was injured, although we all agreed that we had had enough luck for one day.

When we did finally make it to the road, a man in a pickup truck happened by and gave us a ride to town, which seemed disappointingly anticlimactic.

Later, one of the men who had been on this fateful trip stopped in our local newspaper office and told the editor the whole story. The story got written up and, oddly enough, we received quite a bit of business as a result. People would come in to Tex's office and ask, *"Is this the tour that may or may not get back?"*

It was a beautiful day in early July. Tex assigned me to pilot the jet boat to Lathrop Canyon. He and my son Bernie were driving two VW microbuses the fifty miles to the bottom of the canyon. The usual routine was to eat lunch at Lathrop, during which the passengers used the opportunity to compare notes on both the river and land tours. We then swapped passengers for the remainder of the trip. Tex and I liked to change vehicles, too, at the turn-around, so I drove the old, red VW back and Tex piloted the 24-foot jet boat back to his dock. Climbing out of Lathrop Canyon is always a thrill, especially for flatlanders. At first glance, exit from the canyon appears impossible. Halfway up, there is a sharp right turn and the visitor thinks, *"Good heavens, how did I ever get myself into something like this?"* From that point on, everything else is anticlimactic, terrain-wise. The scenery, however, is breathtaking. Musselman Arch, named after a local rancher,

Ross Musselman, is one of the highlights of the trip. Ross came to canyon country from New York around 1930. Later, he acted as a guide for some of the few tourists who were aware that southeastern Utah existed. I've had the good fortune to get to know him and his son Rusty quite well - and so will the reader, in a later chapter.

Musselman Arch   *F.A. Barnes*

Anyway, shortly after leaving the arch, I detected a problem developing with the microbus. It was stuttering badly when I applied the throttle. Since I was in the lead, I decided to take a lower, but still scenic, route rather than attempt to climb the notoriously steep Shafer Trail out of the canyon bottom. This turned out to be a prudent decision because in less than three miles the bus gave up the ghost. I wasn't a bit surprised and had already determined that the culprit was the fuel pump. Luckily, the returning group was smaller than the one in the morning, and we managed to crowd my group in with Bernie's and they headed for Moab. Bernie was to come back to fetch me if I didn't come limping in within an hour or so after he pulled into town. I had a small can of gasoline with me and I poured a little into the

119

carburetor. The engine started right up, verifying my suspicions about the fuel pump. I remembered that there was a small plastic mustard container in the lunch box in the VW. I emptied out the mustard, then rinsed and filled the bottle with gasoline. This was going to act as a miniature gas tank. My next dilemma was where to find a plastic line to run from the mustard bottle to the carburetor, so that I could squeeze the bottle while driving to supply fuel to the VW's carb. I noticed some of the wire for the bus's electrical system was encased in plastic and appeared to be about the right diameter. So I removed the wire from its plastic tubing and fit one end of the tubing to the feed line on the carburetor and the other to the nozzle of the mustard bottle. Fortunately, the tube fit snugly enough that it didn't even leak. I found I could drive about a mile per bottle, then I'd stop, refill the mustard bottle, and go another mile. I even got back to town before Bernie came looking for me! I think I can be forgiven for gloating about my ingenuity on that occasion.

My own jet boat

I worked as a jet boat pilot for Tex for seven years, then started my own jet boat tour business, which I ran until the late 1980s. In the following years, I was semi-retired and ran only infrequent jet boat tours for Jim Sarten and his outfit, North American River Expeditions. We departed at about 8:00 each morning and the boats would be trailered twenty miles down to the Potash Dock and launched.

I had a family of four from Switzerland on one tour. The father spoke broken English; the mother and two children, none at all. Sarten, who ordinarily piloted the boat I was using, had gone to Grand Junction on business and I was on my own if any technical problems occurred while I was on the river. Normally, we experience very few mechanical glitches, since tour operators tend to keep their equipment in good shape.

I gave my usual series of informative lectures to our guests but this group understood very little, so I was trying to "eat the clock," our expression for killing time. The hike into the petrified forests helped pass a good interval, but I soon ran out of things to show and do, so I turned around beyond Dead Horse Point and began the upriver run. I had gone about three miles when I remembered we had some muskmelons on board. I shut down the boat, dug out the melons, and sliced them up. They disappeared rapidly. I took a moment to give my visitors one last view of Dead Horse Point and let them shoot up the rest of their film.

Petrified log

With our little refreshment break over, I prepared to fire up the engine and head back upstream. I hit the key and - click. *"C'mon, you @#$%^&*)!"* Click. Oh, no, not again. I knew that Jim had been having starter problems and carried a spare starter around just in case. I looked high and low, knowing full well it was there somewhere, but I couldn't find it to save my life.

Even when the current is less than 2 mph, it can be a problem jumping off the boat close to shore. There's a slight chance that I would land in deeper water than I anticipated, or that I would be unable to hold the heavy boat in to shore and it would drift off with a load of inexperienced passengers. Risking it, I jumped to the bank and was able to secure the boat. Jim had two batteries aboard, but even hooking both up simultaneously to provide a whopping 24 volts did no good.

After half an hour, I decided to walk up the sheer-walled canyon and see if I could find a place to climb out and go get help. I admit to ulterior motives - I was going crazy sitting there being stared at by folks who couldn't even communicate with me. I hiked to the upper end of the canyon and, seeing no easy way out, considered climbing the sheer wall but got spooked and decided against it. I tried another place that looked promising and wound up on my kiester on a pile of rubble. Okay, I'd been gone over an hour and now I had to plod back and give my rather unreceptive companions the bad news.

About twenty minutes passed. Then I heard a familiar low whine. *"I hear a jet boat coming!"* I yelled excitedly. Of course nobody could decipher what I was babbling, but they caught my mood and knew something good was about to happen. In minutes, Jim Sarten rounded the bend in the river in another of his boats. We were elated to see him and I made darned sure he showed me where that extra starter was hidden in the bow.

People are funny. From all indications I gathered that my passengers didn't exactly have the time of their lives; they seemed kind of sour and I didn't blame them. Being stranded miles from nowhere with some stranger you can't talk to isn't most folks' idea of whoopee. But just before they left in their motor home, the father slipped a ten-dollar tip into my hand!

While traveling in southeastern Utah, one should possess a modicum of survival skills, plenty of emergency equipment, and enough savvy to be able to repair a disabled vehicle on the side of the road.

I had contracted to transport two vehicles down to Lake Powell, so I sub-contracted a friend, Gail Lea, to drive one for me. She drove the Ford Van and I drove the second vehicle with my 1971 Scout 4WD in tow. The Ford had some peculiar quirks which restricted it to a top cruising speed of about 50 mph. It was, therefore, a long trip to Hite Marina, at the north end of the lake. Before starting the 165-mile journey back to Moab in the Scout, we stopped and had a bite to eat. Although it takes a little longer, the return trip via Natural Bridges National Monument and Comb Ridge is quite beautiful. And since I have this habit of not going back the same way as - well, you know. So my victim - er - *friend* and I chose the scenic route.

I know of a nice ruin on the way which can be seen from the road and I wanted to show it to Gail. I stopped to point it out to her but she said she couldn't spot it from where we were parked. So I went to start the car to pull up a little for a better vantage point. The Scout seemed unusually reluctant to start, which worried me quite a bit. I decided, when I finally succeeded in getting it cranked over, that I'd better keep it running in the hope that we'd make it back onto the main highway.

We managed to get to the top of the hill and the engine began running a little better as we approached the entrance to Natural Bridges. I knew it was mostly downhill highway to Comb Wash but I was worried that we wouldn't have the steam to climb Comb Ridge. Sure enough, the Scout began to lose power as we ascended the steep grade. Gail looked at me apprehensively and I felt like a first-class idiot for once again having dragged an innocent bystander along on one of my misadventures. Nevertheless, we chugged along and made it to the summit and started back down the other side. From that point on, I put the Scout in neutral gear at every opportunity. If we could just get to Blanding, we would then have access to a telephone to call my wife and have her send help.

There remained two very steep hills. We conquered the first, despite the deteriorating condition of the engine. Shirt Tail Corner was about six miles ahead and they had a phone, so if we could make that gas station, we could call Moab. I flew down the hill with the throttle wide open, never once backing off. I even negotiated a frighteningly sharp corner with the pedal to the metal. Regardless of my breakneck approach, however, I was losing speed quickly and knew I would never make it to the station. It was a bad place to be stalled - but fortune smiled on us! In about five minutes a friend of mine, Billy Hass, happened along from the other direction in a big tandem gravel truck. He said he would be coming back our way in about twenty minutes and would pull the Scout over the next hill. Not many vehicles were on the road, so, without waiting for Billy, I coasted backward to a turn-around spot and once more got the engine fired up. On the very first try, I made it to the top of the hill I had not been able to climb before and coasted on in to the Shirt Tail Corner gas station. Gail got us a couple of cold drinks while I optimistically filled the gas tank and steeled myself for the 70-plus-mile trip to Moab.

I knew that three miles north of Blanding lay yet another steep hill to climb but, again, by not forcing the throttle too much we were able to master the ascent. It seemed the hill, however, had actually mastered the Scout, because the temperature gauge began to climb into the danger zone and we still had the mother of all hills yet to pull! I quelled my urge to just punch the gas pedal and go flat out until the darn thing blew up. Instead, I judiciously pulled off the road and lifted the hood of the Scout - and immediately wished I HAD just punched the gas pedal and gone flat out until the darn thing blew up! Water was *pouring* out from around the main radiator hose. The flow would have to be stanched quickly or there would be absolutely no coolant left. I was at a loss as to what to do.

We had been standing there, dejectedly, for only about seven or eight minutes when a very attractive young Navajo woman pulled up and asked, *"Can I be of any help?"*

I showed her our trouble and asked her if there was any water at Devils Campground, about two miles away. She offered to go find out. She took our two-gallon water jug and headed north to the campground. I began fabricating a gasket out of some tour-guide brochures that were in the Scout. In a few minutes, still another car driven by a neatly-dressed businessman stopped. Again, *"May I be of any help to you"*?

It turned out that he was on his way down from Salt Lake City on banking business in Blanding. So I gave him my wife's phone number and asked him to call her collect and explain our predicament. We expected to be able to start toward Moab again within about twenty to thirty minutes, but that she should tell our friend, Terry Warner, to head this way anyway just in case we had problems.

Soon, our lovely Navajo benefactress arrived with the water. I had finished making the crude gasket, so I installed it and we shoved off. Whenever possible, I shut the engine off and coasted to conserve coolant and keep our temperature below 200 degrees. The brochure gasket was leaking quite a bit, but we limped another eighteen miles or so into the town of Monticello. Still about fifty miles to go.

"Hey, Gail, you wanna guess where we'll meet Terry on the way out from Moab?"

"How about at the top of Blue Hill?" This is about twelve miles south of Moab. I guessed Wilson Arch, about 25 miles south of Moab. We could see Wilson Arch nearly two miles ahead and the Scout was still rolling along. The gap narrowed to one half mile and still no Terry. We chugged on past Wilson Arch and - here came Terry! I had come about 300 feet from winning the bet. Well, I've never been much of a gambler, but I still consider myself one heck of a shadetree mechanic!

Wilson Arch   F.A. Barnes

CHAPTER SIXTEEN

CLOSE CALLS AND CLOSE COMPANIONS

While visiting friends in California, I heard about a company there that distributed Avon rubber rafts, which I understood were a good, affordable product. So I ordered three of them with the notion of renting them out to tourists hankering for a rafting adventure on the Colorado River. Unfortunately, I didn't know exactly what the ideal size would be for that purpose, and the rafts I purchased were too small, as I later discovered. In addition, my idea was about fifteen years before its time. Rafting on the Colorado is a popular sport in this day and age but, back then, everyone thought I was nuts.

Anyway, my rafts were delivered in late December. Though antsy for a trial run, I restrained myself until mid-January, when it warmed up a mite. I broke out one raft, inflated it, hauled it up the river about ten miles, and cast off. It was sunny and probably in the lower 50s; ordinarily, at this time of year the river is full of ice floes and sometimes so choked with them that the floes have to be dynamited to keep the river from backing up and flooding. Jean was driving along the river road watching my progress. I was enjoying myself immensely - until I came to a shady stretch of water. It hadn't even occurred to me that when I hit these colder spots, the air inside the raft would contract and the raft would go limp. What a surprise! I had hoped to remain on the river until I reached the moderately tame rapids at Big Bend, but with the raft alternating between full and floppy, I decided to call it a day and try again when it warmed up.

In early February, the weather was phenomenal. Temperatures were hitting 60 degrees in the afternoons, so I approached Jean about making a quick raft trip from just upriver of the George White rapids. We had two Volkswagens, one of which we left downriver while we drove the other to the White Ranch to launch the raft. Jean was a little apprehensive as we shoved off into the smooth current. After floating downriver for about a mile, we approached the rapids and put on our life jackets. This was our first real whitewater rafting experience and, with my characteristic 20/20 hindsight, I realize we did some pretty stupid things. Perhaps the worst was that we were sitting too high in the raft. I wanted to get some good 35mm pictures and waited until the last minute to shoot the White Ranch rapid. I took the picture, tossed the camera onto the floor of the raft, then started to back-paddle with the oars. I waited a moment too late; a wave kicked the raft up and all my oar got was air.

Seventy-degree water is too cold for me. But getting instantly dumped into 35-degree water is an incredible shock to the system! After the raft flipped and I surfaced, I looked for Jean and couldn't see her anywhere. The first thing to go through my mind was tomorrow's headline in the Times Independent: Local Jet Boater's Wife Drowns in Colorado River! Little did I know that Jean was in the air pocket underneath the raft, holding on for dear life, but breathing nonetheless and probably in better shape than I was! She soon surfaced near me and swam to the left bank, holding on to an oar for support. I swam for the right bank and pulled the raft with me.

First, I thanked the powers-that-be that we were both still alive. Then I started to shiver and realized that neither of us would last long if I didn't do something quickly. I managed to get the raft turned upright, then scrounged up a tree limb to use as an oar; Jean had one, and the other was probably a mile downriver by now. It took me several minutes to get the raft to the other bank where Jean was. Now, what we had just endured was tough, but it was a piece of cake compared to the struggle I had convincing Jean to get back into the raft for the remaining five miles we still had to float to the other Volkswagen! I can imagine tooth extractions less painful! Luckily, the water on that final stretch was smooth and, as long as we stayed away from the shady spots, the sun slowly began to warm us up.

That trip, combined with my underestimating the size of boat needed, and the fact that no one was very receptive to the concept of raft rentals on the Colorado, kind of put the hex on my little potential business venture. That may have been a blessing in disguise, because I decided shortly afterward to shell out the cash to buy my own jet boat, an investment that proved to be very sound indeed in the years to follow.

I was shooting a Canyonlands National Park video and, since the area I was concentrating on at the time was very primitive, I decided that using the dirt bike to get around would expedite things a bit. Getting in and out of the Doll House section of Canyonlands is arduous. Most of the road is easy with a four-wheel-drive vehicle but there is one area near The Teapot that is extremely rough and I knew the bike would be a much better means of negotiating the sharp curves and steep inclines. With the Scout 4WD, I towed the motorcycle in on a trailer as far as I could comfortably go, then loaded all my gear into my old World War II backpack and strapped my large,

The Doll House   *J.A. Barnes*

heavy tripod across the handlebars. So outfitted, I headed down the road to
the Doll House.

Some of the shots I needed required a certain amount of hiking and
toting of equipment, but it was enjoyable, and by late afternoon I had
wrapped up all the footage I needed. I didn't see another vehicle all day, but
did encounter five backpackers on various trails. My work done, I cranked
up the 185 Suzuki and headed for the Scout, more than forty miles away.
Though I felt a little apprehension as I noticed the sun getting low, I made it
to the Scout before dark. After loading up the bike and stowing my gear, I
happened to feel my hip pocket and immediately realized I had lost my billfold - again! Now, the last time this happened was over fifty years ago, but I
still think that once in a lifetime is often enough for a body to lose his billfold.
I felt like I was getting more than my share of injustice. There's probably
some guy out there who has *never* lost his billfold just because I got his turn!

I thought about going back and looking for it, but then I figured,
*"Nope, somebody'll find it. Anyone who is out here hiking or backpacking is
a different breed from your average city-dweller and will have the decency to
contact me and return my wallet."*

Despite my faith, I worried during the entire drive back to Moab. I
had filled the Scout's gas tank at Hanksville on the way down, but I had only
74 cents in my pocket and didn't think I'd have enough gas to get all the way

home. I took it real easy, trying to conserve fuel; I was sure I could at least get to Green River, where I could call someone if I needed to. Green River came and went. I decided to try for Crescent Junction. I made it with gas to spare. I knew that shooting for Moab, thirty miles away, was stretching it a bit, but I was feeling lucky so I went for it. I made it clear to the downhill stretch coming into Moab when I remembered I had carried a one-quart can of reserve gas on my motorcycle! I stopped just a half-mile north of town and put that last little bit in the tank and it got me to the gas station.

Less than a week later, a fellow from Tucson, Arizona called to say that he had found my wallet and was mailing it to me. Within three days, I received it with everything, including money, intact. Just goes to show what kind of people visit the backcountry. And I guess that getting my wallet back twice kind of makes up for having lost it twice!

I met Mel Dalton in 1956. He was the kind of guy who had a lot of savvy. Mel was dedicated to his family and his church and would go out of his way to help anyone in need. He was a Marine in World War II and later became the Chief of Police of Moab in the late 1960s. Mel did me a good turn once and I feel it deserves at least a brief mention here.

While Jean and I were trying to orchestrate our move from Indiana to Utah, we bought an acre of land in Moab and put a twelve-foot-wide mobile home on it. We were still hopping back and forth between states, and I thought I had shut off and drained all the water lines at the trailer when we left Moab for several weeks during the winter. I was wrong. The lines froze and burst, causing a big mess and what could have been extensive damage had Mel not rounded up a couple of his buddies and gone to work fixing the lines and cleaning up the flood.

For several years prior to Mel's being appointed Chief of Police, Ken Aiken held that post. Ken and his wife Alice used to live in Estes Park, Colorado, but decided to move to California. I never found out what prompted them to leave Interstate 70 and drive thirty miles south to Moab while they were en route to California, but I sure am glad they did. The uranium boom was in full swing and Moab was a hopping little town. Ken and Alice decided they liked it so much that they stayed and went to work for the telephone company.

Ken was an avid 16mm camera buff and he and Alice went out into the canyon country at every opportunity. They had a British Land Rover and, since four-wheel-drive vehicles weren't too common back then, they soon knew more about Moab's backcountry than most of the locals. They were enthusiastic, vivacious people and we enjoyed many trips with them into the wilderness.

One day Alice and Ken came over and invited us to accompany them on a camping trip in Canyonlands. They had been wanting to introduce us to a special hideaway. Jean and I were excited; we had been wanting to go into that area but didn't know the region well enough to try it on our own. Well, you know what they say about the best-laid plans. A few days before the trip, Ken went into the bathroom to shave. Alice heard a thud and rushed into the bathroom to find her beloved Ken lying dead on the floor, having suffered a massive heart attack. On the day Ken was supposed to visit his favorite spot in the wilderness he was, instead, guest of honor at a funeral. I miss him to this day.

Moab was just beginning to show some signs of becoming a tourist attraction. Of course, these changes necessitated an upgrading of the police department and sheriff's office. Several more law enforcement officers were hired, and among these was Dan Ison, a cop from Denver. Dan fit right in. He was very professional, and had a strong sense of community. He was also an avid four-wheeling enthusiast and he and I hit it off immediately. His wife was also named Jean and the "pair of Jeans" became fast friends, too. The four of us spent quite a bit of time together and the two gals put up with a lot of foolishness from us. The following is an example.

At about nine o'clock on a Saturday morning I stopped by Dan's house. We started chatting and somehow I got on the subject of an old Chinese bathtub that had been built by coolies who had worked on the railroad in the late 1800s. Like most people around here, he had never heard anything about it. He hadn't been to Crystal Geyser either, so I suggested we take a trip out to see these two unusual features. Dan was all for it. His Jean made us a couple of sandwiches, I checked in with my Jean, and soon we were on our way in the Scout 4WD.

The Chinese bath is very close to old U.S. 6, but not easy to locate. It consists of a cement tank, about nine feet square and thirty inches deep, with the bottom tapered toward the middle, although no drain is evident. We ogled it for a while, then drove on to the geyser. I had been to the geyser dozens of times and so had a pretty good idea of when it was to erupt. This

Crystal Geyser

trip, we hit it right on the money and got some great video footage of the 30-minute display.

Well, that quest only took a little while and we weren't really ready to head back to town yet. An idea occurred to me.

"Dan, have you ever been to the Maze?" I asked. The Maze is a district in western Canyonlands which lives up to its name. It was only eighty miles to the Maze ranger station from where we were. I didn't have to twist his arm. When we got to the ranger station, I asked about the condition of the notorious Flint Trail. To my surprise, the ranger told us that the road had just been bladed and was perfectly passable in a four-wheel-drive. Well, he was right. The Flint Trail was in great shape but the trail beyond it was lousy. I kept thinking it had to get better up ahead, but it didn't. By this time, we had reached the point of no return and were committed to another thirty-some-odd miles of rugged dirt trail that would lead us out to Utah 95 near Hite Marina on Lake Powell. The sun was rapidly going behind the cliffs, so I switched on the lights. Nothing got any brighter.

"Dan, I don't think our lights are working," I observed with my customary brilliance. We drove to a high point and shut off the engine. From its failure to restart, we deduced that there was a little problem with the battery, so we disconnected the cables and cleaned the battery terminals. With our fingers crossed, we hopped back in the Scout and coasted down the hill. The bump start was exactly that - bumpy - but we got 'er running and the battery seemed to be taking a charge. We made it to Hanksville at about 11:00 p.m. and called the pair of Jeans to let them know we'd be home in another three hours or so. What a day!

Jean and I decided to head down to Lake Powell with the Isons. We were in Dan's Bronco and had stopped at a gas station to refuel. While waiting for Dan to finish, Jean and I sauntered around to the rear of the gas station and shot some videotape of a big hot air balloon that was tethered to the ground. The balloonist offered Jean and me a ride, although we would be restricted to the full length of the tether. We hopped in the basket and the guy fired up the burner to get us off the ground, scorching my poor old bald head in the process! We floated around on our leash for a while, then he brought us back down. It was a novel experience for us but we decided that fifty feet off the ground was plenty high enough for us. Little did we imagine at that time that such a sport as bungee-jumping from such balloons would develop years later. Even Moab boasts such an activity today.

On the way to Lake Powell, one passes through the teeming metropolis of Hanksville, Utah. Except for a couple of gas pumps, I don't think Hanksville has changed much since Butch Cassidy and his nefarious bunch hung out there. I've read someplace that Hanksville can boast having the greatest fluctuation in temperature range of any town in the continental United States; the low being 50 degrees below zero in the winter and the high being around 120 degrees in the summer. I don't know about the low, but I have no doubt that the high is not exaggerated one iota! Anyway, I guess every little one-horse town in the country has to be able to brag about being unique in some way, and there's not a heck of a lot else to set Hanksville apart from all the others. I think somebody probably had to think pretty hard to come up with that little tidbit.

To the west of Hanksville lie the Henry Mountains, a range named after one of the founders of the Smithsonian Institution. Over the past hundred years or so, the Henrys have gone by many names. In the 1870s,

Bungee jumping near Moab, 1992   F.A. Barnes

they were referred to as the "Broken Alkaline Mountains"; later, they were called the "No Name Mountains," a designation obviously assigned them by someone of unparalleled originality. Probably the same guy who drew the map I once saw showing Moab in Paiute County rather than Grand County, where it is today. Kind of hard to swallow that Moab would just get up and move to another county like that once it discovered it was in the wrong place, but then you never know about these Utah towns.

Back to the journey to Lake Powell. When the newcomer finally catches sight of the lake itself, after having traveled through 160 miles of the driest desert known to man, he naturally assumes it's a mirage. Common sense tells him that all that sapphire blue water simply cannot exist in such a brutal, desolate region. But there it is. And it's real. One hundred and

Lake Powell and Navajo Mountain   F.A. Barnes

eighty miles long and scores of side canyons to explore. With sheer rock walls rising hundreds of feet from the water line in many places, Lake Powell is a truly spectacular recreational area.

After reaching the lake and exploring around a bit, we discussed the route we'd take on our return trip. Dan and I didn't give the Jeans much of a choice - deciding with what we considered a majority vote to go through "The Bear's Ears." We were pretty sure we had enough gas to get at least as far as Dugout Ranch, where we could probably get some more in a pinch. So we took off up the incline toward the saddle between the two rock outcroppings which look, from a distance, exactly like a bear's ears. The elevation at this swag is about 8,000 feet, a height which provides a breathtaking view of Arch Canyon and the surrounding territory. The trail climbs to about 9,000 feet before descending through "The Notch" into Beef Basin, where it levels off and heads in a westerly direction. We made a left turn and visited the Anasazi dwelling where I had found the metate ten years before. The ancients had left their fingerprints embedded in the mud mortar of the dwelling's walls, where they can still be seen.

We were all wishing we could spend the night in these pristine surroundings, but we had to leave if we were to make the stops we wanted to and still get back to Moab. We climbed back into the Bronc and drove about five miles west and a mile south to still more Anasazi ruins. These ruins, though all in the same general vicinity, were of different ages. We got out of the Bronco and walked about seventy feet to one well-preserved structure. After looking at it for a while, I figured out what was nagging at the back of my mind.

"Hey Jean, do you see anything unusual in the window of that ruin?" I asked.

At first she didn't know what I meant. All she saw was a window in a ruin. Then I pointed to a wooden rod running across the top of the window and her eyes widened in recognition. I swear this Indian ruin had curtain rods! The ancients were even more civilized than we thought!

It was mid-afternoon and we had a challenging trek ahead of us. Descending the notorious Bobby's Hole trail is not a venture for the faint of heart. S.O.B. Hill can make anyone quake in their boots, but it's a mere introduction to the back side of Elephant Hill. Dan demonstrated his four-wheeling prowess, muscling the Bronco up, over, and down the other side of the hill. After passing Dugout Ranch, we stopped at the famous Newspaper Rock, probably the most concentrated exhibit of petroglyphs in the Four Corners area. We came back onto U.S. 191, about forty miles south of Moab and finally coasted into town on the fumes left in the gas tank.

Newspaper Rock   F.A. Barnes

CHAPTER SEVENTEEN

THE CANYON KING

Tex met Cap'n Jim Binkley on a trip to Fairbanks, Alaska. I don't know what Tex was doing in Alaska, and I never asked him. But he must have impressed the daylights out of Cap'n Jim with his tales of Canyonlands, because Jim decided to fly on down to the "lower 48" and see for himself. Now, Jim was an airplane pilot and a riverboat man, operating big paddlewheelers out of Fairbanks, and he knew rivers like nobody's business. Well, sure enough, he takes one look at the Colorado River and pretty soon he and Tex are shut up inside Tex's office drawing up plans for a 93-foot sternwheeler!

Work began on the "Canyon King" the first week in January 1971. Many locals considered it the most harebrained scheme they'd ever heard of - another "Fulton's Folly." Some thought it would be a great boon to the tourist industry. Others simply withheld judgment and decided to just wait and see what happened. In the last week of April, several hundred people participated in the christening and launching of the huge craft. The launch ramp was covered with straw for several hundred feet up the slope, and ropes and pulleys were rigged for sliding the boat over the straw, down the ramp and into the water. Everyone heaved mightily on the ropes, but ultimately a big bulldozer was needed to get the immense craft launched.

Launching the CANYON KING   F.A. Barnes

Utah's Governor Calvin Rampton speaking prior to the maiden voyage of the CANYON KING

G.A. Barnes

Several weeks later, following a trial run and more outfitting, Utah's Governor Calvin Rampton joined us for the maiden voyage - which was shortstopped by a sandbar after a mile or so! While a chagrined Cap'n Tex feverishly conducted extrication procedures with a couple of small-boat pilots, Frenchie LeForrest kept the passengers preoccupied with music on his portable organ. The crowd joined in singing, ate their brown-bag lunches, and had a good visit. Before the boat floated free almost two hours later,

Governor Rampton's presence was required on shore for another appointment. He was off-loaded into a small boat and taken to shore, and thence to Arches where he was to dedicate the Monument as a National Park. When the Canyon King finally floated free, great hurrahs went up from the festive crowd and the trip proceeded without further ado.

The spring runoff had just started, but the river was rising more rapidly than in a usual runoff. Tex had temporarily docked his big triple-engined jet boat at the Potash ramp. When the water level came up unexpectedly, the moorings broke and the big boat headed downriver, unmanned! Luckily, a park ranger happened to be on the river in his outboard, conducting a desert bighorn sheep survey, and saw this huge boat coming down the river with neither pilot nor passengers aboard. Using his little outboard and no little effort, he managed to secure the runaway monster. He then radioed headquarters and asked them to contact Tex to let him know he was missing a boat. The ranger said that he would stay with the jet boat until Tex got there to take over the show.

F.A. Barnes

The paddlewheeler, Canyon King, was docked near the river bridge and was the only boat Tex had that was big enough and powerful enough to tow the big jet boat back upstream, so Tex got her fired up. He called me and asked me to come along and bring my small jet boat as a backup in case of problems. I had to do a little work on my jet boat, so I told him I'd catch up with him somewhere around Dead Horse Point. I asked my wife Jean, my daughter Elaine, her husband and a couple of friends, Bertha and Dick Reynolds, if they'd like to come along. They accepted. Before long, I had my jet boat launched and on the way, but we had trouble with a vapor lock and spent about 45 minutes correcting the situation. With the very high water, we could travel swiftly without having to worry about sandbars. Even so, we didn't catch up with Tex until we were fifty miles downriver and night was upon us. We were lucky to have a small sliver of moon to see by. When we reached the spot where the big jet was moored, we made the truant craft secure to the port side of the paddlewheeler, lashed the ranger's boat and my little jet to the starboard side, and headed back upriver. The Canyon King only made about 1 to 1-1/2 mph with the weight it was dragging.

The entire ordeal up to this point had taken most of the night. It was starting to get light and we were still nowhere near our destination. My son-in-law had to be in Moab by 7:00 a.m. to open his grocery store, so I put him and Elaine in my little jet, cast off from the paddlewheeler, and sped upriver to take them to the dock where they had parked their car. A very weary Tex and company straggled in well after noon.

Tragically, the following week, the young ranger who had rescued the big boat was killed in a plane crash with my pilot friend, Dick Smith, and two other rangers while conducting an aerial bighorn sheep survey.

F.A. Barnes

CHAPTER EIGHTEEN

FAVORITE STOMPING GROUNDS

With the opening of the Texas Gulf potash mine downriver from Moab came the construction of a beautiful new stretch of highway along the Colorado River. In addition, a railroad was built for transporting the potash out to the main highway thirty miles away. In order to maintain a consistent gradient, a 7,000-foot tunnel was cut through native rock for the railroad. This tunnel was blasted out from both ends and met in the middle. While the potash plant was being built, there was no easily passable access road to the plant site - only a dirt trail - and dozens of outboard boats transported the construction workers to and from the site. By 1962, the new highway along the river was finished. The pavement ended at the potash plant, but a dirt road continued on for several miles, eventually climbing up the Shafer Trail to the Island-in-the-Sky. A traveler can take a branch off to the right just beyond Jughandle Arch, and follow Long Canyon up over Pucker Pass and thence to Utah 313, the road to Dead Horse Point.

Long Canyon *F.A. Barnes*

I first followed this road in 1956, long before Jean and I moved from Indiana to Utah. It was a very rough and dusty trip over the unimproved dirt road and it nearly beat my 1955 Chevy sedan to pieces, but the excitement of penetrating the wild region was worth the ride. In the winter of 1957, I took my wife and two kids, ages six and seven, all the way down the river road to the MGM (Monte G. Mason) oil wells, which first began producing in 1955. For some very interesting reading about this trail up to Mason's oil wells, I recommend issue number 14 of the <u>Canyon Legacy</u>, the journal of the Dan O'Laurie Museum in Moab. Huge barges were used to get the exploration and drilling equipment to the site.

The MGM venture was not the first attempt at locating oil in this area. On Christmas day in 1926, the Midwest Oil Company hit a producing well in the same general area. The well blew out and it took several weeks to extinguish the fire.

When I first started cruising the Colorado River with my outboard in the early 1960s, I would go ashore and rummage around in the remains of the buildings at the well site. There were many old outboard parts lying around and I scrounged some and cleaned them up for spares. Later, when I became a jet boat tour guide with Tex, I frequently made stops there. One of my tricks was to open a valve on the well and show my guests how the high grade oil would squirt out of the pipe.

Anyway, back to the trip with my wife and kids on this beautiful winter day. Oblivious to what lay beyond, we toodled on down the dirt road past where the potash plant now operates. At this juncture, we were not destined to experience Pucker Pass, but we did negotiate some pretty rough country in that old '55 Chevy. Looking back, it's a wonder we made it as far as we did, and a blessing that we didn't take the Long Canyon branch to Pucker Pass, because with that street vehicle we may never have come back out again. We did, however, reach a viewpoint some 200 feet above the MGM oil operation, overlooking the wells. Surprisingly, the trail beyond the wells wasn't too bad. We had been on top of Dead Horse Point and recognized it as we passed below it. Our first really steep climb after passing under Dead Horse Point brought us to a fantastic overlook of the Colorado River. Here, the road narrowed considerably. We shot a bunch of pictures, then drove another ten minutes or so until we located a good lunch spot with an incredible view of a huge bend in the river.

Soon, we were at the bottom of the Shafer Trail, looking up at several precarious switchbacks and deciding whether or not to brave the climb. The Shafer Trail, named after brothers Frank and John "Sog" Shafer, is a passage once used by cattlemen and sheepherders who wanted a more direct route from the lowlands to the mesa above, now known as the Island-in-the-Sky. It was later improved and used by mining outfits. Today the Shafer Trail functions primarily as a thrillingly scenic tourist route. The area in which it lies is now within Canyonlands National Park, so the road is kept in fairly good condition.

After a grueling climb up the steep, narrow switchbacks of the trail, with its appalling views back toward the Colorado River gorge, we reached the summit of the trail and, with great relief, drove out into open terrain of the Island-in-the-Sky. On the maps, this broad, relatively level area is divided into two pastures, the south one referred to as Gray's Pasture, so named because of a gray horse that was kept there for years. The north one is known as Arth's Pasture, after rancher Arthur Taylor. We continued north for several miles, then angled east, descending into Sevenmile Canyon, and then on to meet U.S. 191, about nine miles north of Moab. After a full day's travel on rough, dirt roads, Jean and the kids had had enough and were ready to call it a day.

In 1957, Pucker Pass was not so labeled on most Government topographical maps, but anyone making the trip up or down Long Canyon soon became acquainted with this rugged stretch of trail and understood why it bore the nickname. In the early days, the pass was known as Shipman's Cutoff. Jay Roberts, a local equipment operator, upgraded the trail through Long Canyon at one point, but it still remains a challenge.

My first trip up Long Canyon and over Pucker Pass was during one of my visits to Moab in 1961. I had just bought a two-wheel-drive International Travelall. Even though the road was not well-maintained at the time, it was in good enough condition for two-wheel-drive vehicles with good clearance, as mine had.

In 1962, while I was still living in Indianapolis, my friend Harry Grinstead and I loaded our dirt bikes onto Harry's motorcycle trailer, hitched the trailer up to a Chevy Corvair that we had rigged up with a bumper hitch, and headed west to Utah. Taking turns at the wheel, we drove straight through. I had told Harry about the interesting cold water geyser just south of the town of Green River, Utah, so we passed up the Moab turnoff and went on to the geyser. We arrived sometime after 2:00 a.m. and caught a few winks about 300 feet from the geyser, not wanting to miss it when it erupted. Well, of course, you've heard of the watched pot that never boils. Harry and I got up early the next morning and stood around waiting for that doggone geyser to go off. Had we not been there, it probably would have spouted right on schedule. As it was, we waited until well after 9:00 o'clock that morning and finally gave up and drove to Moab.

That afternoon, I took Harry out to the MGM oil wells where the drilling was still in progress. After checking it out, we drove five miles to Pucker Pass and started down steeply curving Long Canyon. As we rounded the first sharp turn to the left, we saw two women and four children walking up the steep slope, one of the women carrying a tiny baby! Stunned, I asked them how they came to be there. They said their Rambler couldn't make it up the hill and had stalled in the steepest place. They could neither back it down nor turn it around, so they had decided to try walking back to Moab. Harry and I got their car turned around for them and sent the ladies and kids on back down the hill safely and we continued on our way.

I always look forward to going out into the high desert to cut wood, and Pucker Pass was one of my favorite trips. It was late November and I needed about one more pickup truck load to carry us through the winter months. Jean was busy that day, so I went alone. It's only four miles from the potash road turnoff to the top of Pucker Pass, although it seems much farther. I knew there had been a few light snowfalls down around 5,000 feet, so I wasn't too surprised to see some patches of the white stuff when I got into the shady areas. The first few skiffs of snow I encountered were only an inch or so deep and I roared right on through them. Then I came onto a three-incher. Well, that was still no problem - until the whole rig began sliding backward down the hill! Brakes are useless in a situation like this one, so I held my breath until the vehicle stopped sliding - in this instance, after about a foot or two. I learned my lesson about taking snow on steep surfaces too lightly.

The next time I found myself in a fix on Pucker Pass was in autumn. I had gone up toward the Pass area early one morning, by way of paved Utah 313, to get a load of firewood. I also planned to collect some flat rock for a wall I was building around our house. I had the 1970 Scout pulling a fairly long trailer built from a 3/4-ton pickup and, behind that, another trailer built from a 1/2-ton pickup.

It was a fruitful trip and I had about a ton of rock in the front trailer and a full load of pinyon pine in the second trailer. From experience, I knew it would be quicker if I returned to Moab the way I had come - but I got greedy. I thought that maybe I would find a few more nice flat rocks if I went down the Pucker Pass/Long Canyon trail (obviously a classic case of the rocks being nicer and flatter on the other side of the hill). Up on the mesa, I was cruising along at about 15 mph. Then when I neared the very steep grade, I dropped down into low range. Once past that stretch, I shifted up a gear, so that I could come on down a little faster. I regularly checked my mirrors to make sure both trailers were all right. Well, I guess my checks became a little too infrequent, because I glanced back and suddenly discovered that I was missing the rear trailer with the load of wood on it!

"Holy Smoke!" I hollered, knowing for sure the dang thing had taken a swan dive off that 400-foot drop I'd just passed. Since the road is, basically, still a trail in many places, I had to wait for a suitable spot to pull off and disconnect the remaining trailer so I could turn around and go back up to survey the damage. When I rounded a bend and spotted my trailer in a shallow ditch, I breathed a sigh of relief. Using my Handyman jack, I managed to get the trailer out of the ditch and hooked back up to the Scout. Then I drove back down to the rock trailer, unhitched the wood trailer, hitched up the rock trailer, then re-hitched the wood trailer on the back again. By this time I was ready to shove the whole lot of them off the cliff and walk to town, but I got myself calmed down and successfully brought the entire rig back home.

Pucker Pass summit

F.A. Barnes

144

CHAPTER NINETEEN

DIRT BIKE DIDOES

February is one of my favorite months in Canyonlands. The days are starting to get a little longer and the weather a little warmer. At this time of year, though, elevation still determines where you can go and where you can't.

I was still in bed when I got a call from my friend Bob Jones, of Tag-a-Long Tours. *"Hey, Fred, the Marlboro guys want to go on a backcountry motorcycle tour. Can you take us out today?"* Well, he didn't have to ask twice. I got my riding togs together and hit the trail.

They had several 800cc BMW bikes, and my old 185cc Suzuki was drastically outclassed as we headed north, but with a 55-mph speed limit on U.S. 191, they had to follow their leader. About eight miles out, we turned left across the railroad tracks, then picked up a well-maintained dirt trail that led us up to a fabulous viewpoint where we could see Moab valley, Arches National Park, and the La Sal Mountains beyond. The northernmost segment of Arches National Park is Eagle Park, which can only be experienced on foot. South of Eagle Park is the Dark Angel, then Devils Garden with its concentration of huge and unusual arches. Landscape Arch is the most magnificent and longest of these. From our viewpoint, however, we could only see one arch, Skyline Arch, at the end of the Fiery Furnace trail.

The Gooney Bird,
Little Canyon
F.A. Barnes

Back on the motorbikes, we descended into Little Canyon, in which the outstanding feature is a huge rock prominence known as the "Gooney Bird." Little Canyon is about 2-1/2 miles long. We climbed out of the canyon, then continued on the route to the Gemini Bridges, two spectacular twin natural spans, one measuring 89 feet across, and the other, 70.5 feet. This trail forks not far beyond Little Canyon, the left branch leading to the base of Gemini Bridges, the right to the top of them.

We kept climbing steadily and were now at an elevation of about 5,700 feet when we reached the top of the bridges. Some snow still remained in the shade beneath trees and rocks. Our tracks were the only ones laid there in a long time.

There are several interesting but conflicting stories about who first discovered these phenomenal rock spans. The Taylor family has run cattle in this area, and in parts of what is now Canyonlands National Park, for decades. Arthur Taylor, better known as Arth, was perhaps the earliest of his clan to have become familiar with this region, and claimed to have known of the existence of the bridges for years. My friend, Jimmie Walker, said the Gemini Bridges were first seen by members of the Stewart family, who had dubbed them "The Stewart Twins." In the mid-fifties, Lin Ottinger came to Moab from Tennessee and established his tour business. Several years later, on one of his exploratory hikes into the boonies, he meandered up Abe Day Canyon and stumbled upon the Gemini Bridges. However, their location was so remote that Lin "misplaced" them for eleven years, until 1968 when, with some determination, he again found the site. Fran Barnes, Lin's friend and companion on this trip, wrote the Board on Geographic Names, giving them all the particulars; and in March 1969 the Board officially granted the name "Gemini Bridges" to the two spectacular spans. See Barnes' book *Canyon Country* ARCHES & BRIDGES for the details of re-finding and measuring the bridges.

Back to the bike ride. Our riders thought they had a fabulous view of Arches when we first left U.S 191, but as we climbed another 800 feet, we could see the Book Cliffs in the north, the Uncompahgre Plateau in Colorado to the east, the nearby La Sal Mountains, and the Abajo Mountains fifty miles to the south, near Monticello. The only fairly proximate mountains we couldn't see were the Henry range about seventy miles east, near Hanksville.

As an encore, we decided to ride out the Dead Horse Point State Park road, then cut off after about three miles and head down Long Canyon via Pucker Pass. We stopped at a couple of the more captivating viewpoints,

Gemini Bridges   F.A. Barnes

then began a steep descent and suddenly found ourselves in six inches of snow! Now, I had never biked Pucker Pass and Long Canyon in real snow before and, believe me, I was more than impressed. I was downright scared! Despite my trepidation at the prospect of descending this snow-packed trail, I had to act nonchalant lest my companions become uneasy. At this point there was no turning back, either. However, once I took the initiative and started across the snow, everyone else followed and they all did a remarkable job of maneuvering the big bikes down the steep, slippery slope. Happily, everyone made it all the way out to the river road without incident.

In the past few years, mountain biking has become an increasingly favored sport, especially here in canyon country. In fact, it has become so popular that many mountain bikers now feel that they have exclusive rights to this territory and consider themselves the discoverers of "slickrock." Wrong, amigos! You're about 25 years late, although we do welcome you to share our love for the smooth, rolling sandstone we call slickrock.

In 1962, I first rode a two-stroke dirt bike over most of what is now the Slickrock Bike Trail. My writer friend, Dick Wilson, had shown me this marvelous but little-known expanse of slickrock that was absolutely perfect for two-wheelers, and I ended up taking many of my friends up there to ride. My son Bernie was beginning to take an interest in motorcycles at that time and accompanied me on many occasions.

I once had an interesting experience with a young man who rode the trail with me several years ago. On more than one occasion, it seemed to me that he just hopped off the bike and deliberately let it fall over a ledge; sometimes these drops were well over ten feet. I couldn't for the life of me understand why he was mistreating a perfectly good motorcycle that belonged to his father. Finally, this bothered me so much that I pinned him down and asked him why he seemed bent on destroying the bike.

"But Fred, there aren't any brakes on this bike!" He answered. I guess if he hadn't let the bike go, he would have gone over, too!

Scenic stretch, Slickrock Bike Trail   *F.A. Barnes*

148

In 1966, the Bureau of Land Management officially demarcated and publicized the trail for dirt bike use. At first traffic was sparse, but it soon increased. Then a fatality occurred in which a novice rider on a 90cc Suzuki missed a turn at the north end of the trail and drove off a 600-foot drop. This clearly demonstrated that the trail needed more obvious markings directing and regulating bike traffic. The BLM immediately improved the markings and, of the thousands of motorcyclists and bicyclists who have used the trail since that time, few have suffered serious accidents.

Even after numerous visits to Moab, my Canadian buddy, Gordon Sherley, still had trouble believing that we had the kind of weather that would permit us to ride dirt bikes in the middle of winter. One sunny January day, we packed a lunch, fired up the bikes, and headed up the Slickrock Bike Trail. After riding the marked trail for a few hours, I suggested that we eat lunch and then shoot off on a jeep trail that wound around and ended up on an overlook offering a great view of Moab valley. We unpacked the lunch and fell to. While we were eating and chatting, we observed some lengths of explosive cord lying around and thought it looked like someone might be getting ready to do some blasting nearby. This being mining country, we didn't think much of it and we felt fairly secure in the knowledge that nobody would be dumb enough to blast near a marked trail.

We finished lunch and headed north toward the jeep trail. We had to stop and open a cattle gate to gain access and, once more, we saw explosive cord. This time, it was strung across the trail and we rode right over it. After a bit, we left the main trail and headed across the Navajo sandstone and down into a canyon. In the canyon, we saw four guys sitting in the sun, eating their lunch. They seemed really surprised to see us come riding up; apparently, they hadn't expected anyone to be in the vicinity. They explained that they were part of a mining venture and that we had happened into the middle of their blasting operation. In a few minutes, they said, a charge would be going off. We told them that we were headed north to the Colorado River overlook and wouldn't be in the area long. About that time, the ground shook from a blast which turned out to have been carried by the cord we had just run over! Not wishing to seem rude, we chatted a few minutes more and then got the heck out of there.

In a few minutes we were at the Colorado River overlook, the same cliff made famous by the amateur dirt-biker who had done the unsuccessful Evel Knievel impression on his flying Suzuki. I guess those miners didn't want us to get too relaxed, because we crossed another length of primer cord along the way and heard the blast a few seconds after we ran over that cord!

Gordon must have been pretty impressed with this wintertime biking, because he decided to return the following February. There's an area beyond Castle Valley, Fisher Valley, and Onion Creek called "Top of the World." Gordon had ridden Onion Creek many times and always gazed wistfully to the east toward the Top of the World, so we decided that, on this trip, we'd make it all the way. It took us a good part of the day to reach the lofty overlook and, boy, is it spectacular! Now, I had to laugh. Gord flew jet airplanes every day at over 30,000 feet with no problem, but this little ol' 7,000-foot cliff really spooked him!

Top-of-the-World, above Fisher Valley   *F.A. Barnes*

A young lady named Carol had come with us on her 100cc bike. She was an excellent rider, but had a heart problem that manifested itself at high altitudes. Had I been aware of her ailment, I surely would have discouraged her from coming along on this particular trip. There was a little snow on the summit of Top of the World and, oddly enough, its depth increased as we descended. I ended up riding Carol's bike back through the deep snow to a clear area where she could take over and ride it on out to a lower elevation. She and Gordon waited down on the flat while I waded back through the deep snow to get my bike. By that time, I was plumb tuckered. The sun was getting lower but we managed to make good time, dropping several hundred feet in elevation on an excellent graveled road that led us to the Dewey Bridge and Utah 128, which was paved all the way back to Moab.

I had to deliver a pickup truck to Hite, Utah, so I decided to put my Suzuki in the bed of the truck and ride the bike back to Moab via the scenic route, once I had completed the delivery. Often, river runners hire someone to drive a shuttle vehicle down to Hite, which is the stopping point for the Cataract Canyon raft trip. The usual route is west on Interstate 70 to twelve miles west of Green River, then south to Hanksville on Utah 24, then Utah 95 to Hite on Lake Powell. However, a recent flash flood had washed out enough of the road to Hite that it was impossible to go beyond the turnoff to Bullfrog Marina. So I opted for the other route, directly south from Moab through Monticello, Blanding, and Fry Canyon, which is actually more scenic. I planned to return the usual way, as I was sure I could make it past the washout on my dirt bike.

Whenever I make the return trip from Lake Powell, I rarely know for sure where I'm going to wind up. Now, I'm always quick to advise visitors not to travel alone in the backcountry but, often as not, I fail to heed my own words because I so love to explore. I do, however, always take the precaution of carrying a couple of days' worth of water, and matches in a waterproof container. The importance of water in the desert requires no explanation. The matches can come in very handy for more than just building a fire to keep warm at night or to cook over. In an extreme emergency, for example, an injury that would restrict one's ability to ride or walk out, the matches can be used to set a tire on fire. This, of course, produces very thick, black smoke which can be seen from quite a distance.

Back to my trip. Right after I crossed the San Rafael River, I spotted a trail that led off to the east and decided to follow it. After about six miles, though, it seemed to peter out. This didn't bother me too much, as I knew that if I continued my easterly heading I would eventually reach the Green River. I also knew there was a dirt road in that vicinity that went south to A. C. Ekker's Ranch, so I would be able to reach the town of Green River in either case.

When I finally did make Green River, I topped off the gas tank and got a bite to eat before heading for Moab. I decided to take the old highway which parallels the Interstate but soon discovered that my way was barred by a locked gate. I had seen a dirt trail which turned off the old highway and looked like it led toward Ruby Ranch, so I turned back and followed that one. After several miles, I encountered another locked gate and turned back, taking yet another, less-used side trail, hoping that it was gateless and that it went in the general direction I wanted to go.

Pretty soon, I ended up in a low spot where I could see no landmarks, not even the La Sal Mountains. The sun was directly overhead, so that gave me no help whatsoever. By that time, I had run out of trail - and almost out of water - and was feeling awfully stupid, not to mention lost and thirsty. Despite all these adverse conditions, however, I still had a gut feeling I was going in the right direction and would eventually stumble on either the Ruby Ranch road or an old oil well road to the east of Ruby Ranch. I persevered, and soon came out on the Ruby Ranch road, following it to a power line trail, then tracing the power line trail all the way back to Highway 191 and on to Moab. The trip took several hours longer than it should have and taught me some important lessons, namely, that I was not immune to the treachery of the desert, and that I should follow my own good advice with respect to traveling alone and carrying plenty of water.

Playing around on the dunes

It was early October and Tex and I had closed the jet boat tour business down for the winter. Mel Swanson came over to Tex's place one morning and asked me if I'd like to be his partner in an 8-hour motorcycle race outside Grand Junction, Colorado the following week. It sounded too good to pass up.

The race was open to any size motorcycle. It was sponsored by an "outlaw" club so the rules of the American Motorcycle Association did not apply. The race was to start promptly at 8:00 a.m. Two riders would be registered per bike. The riders would take turns riding the bike and could switch off whenever they wanted to.

Mel asked if I wanted to come over and ride his 250cc Greeves a little to get the feel of it. I confidently told him that I had been riding bikes a long time and doubted if another week of practice would improve my ability any.

The following Saturday, we left Moab before daybreak and rolled into the starting area about 7:00 a.m. All kinds of bikes and riders were there. We unloaded and checked in to pay our entrance fee and find out about any last-minute changes that may have taken place. Most of the bikes had 250cc to 350cc engines and some were mighty exotic! Since AMA rules didn't apply, it turned out that a few guys had mixed up some really potent fuel concoctions and even carried spare engines around with them to swap during the race. Mel and I decided we would change riders every four laps with each lap being about three miles long. We later realized that we should have run at least eight laps apiece before changing over.

I was ready for Mel when he pulled in for the first rider change-over. I'd developed a case of butterflies by then, but they subsided quickly once I got rolling. Everything went fine until I came to the end of my own first four laps, which seemed all too soon, and arrived at the pit area at too hot a pace. I made a quick grab for the brake handle - and was promptly vaulted head first over the handlebars! I had never ridden a bike with such a good front brake before! As Mel was picking up the bike, I yelled at him, "I'm not sure I can ride anymore. I feel terrible - and I think I might have broken my hip bone!" Even if I hadn't been in such pain, I'd probably have been much too humiliated to even get back on the bike again.

However, while I waited for Mel to finish his next four laps, I began to feel a little better and decided to go ahead with the race. It seemed to take about an hour and a half to really get into the swing of this new type of racing. We had no sure way of determining how we stood until we were about two hours into the race. My rough guess was that we were very close to last place. Our old "thumper" was serving us well, though, and I was getting used to those Earles front forks.

About three hours into the race, we noticed frantic activity taking place in several of the pits of the better riders. We found out later that one team was using their third engine! Our bike was still running extremely well when we finished the first four hours.

At this point, we were shuttled off onto an entirely new 4-mile course on very uneven Mancos Shale. The undulating terrain made for alternating better visibility so we knew when we could really pour it on and when we'd have to take it easy. The leading bike was in the process of passing me and I decided to drop in behind him and see what he was doing that I wasn't. Very soon, I determined how he was beating us. There was one distinct jump - whoop-dee-doo - on the track. I went into this at full throttle behind a 350cc special motocross bike. It scared me to death but I learned something! I never again backed off the throttle on this one rise, and soon started passing riders like they were standing still. Pretty soon, we were moving up on the faster riders - and actually finished up the race in fourth place out of thirty machines! I was ecstatic, even though it did take me three weeks to get over my hip injury!

Airborne!   *J.A. Barnes*

CHAPTER TWENTY

CRUSTY CHARACTERS AND HISTORICAL HIDEOUTS

Not quite two miles downriver from Moab is Kings Bottom. Twenty-seven miles upriver from Moab, etched in a big boulder beside what is now Utah 128, are the words "King's Toll Road." Apparently, the river road, as we now refer to it, used to be a crude toll road which led to a crossing where a Mr. King operated a ferry service. This presumably provided transport for livestock and wagons to the other side of the Colorado River near where Dewey Bridge now stands. Mr. King must have been a pretty enterprising fellow to have owned a lucrative ferry business, had a toll road named after him, and had a bottom (other than the one he sat on) also bearing his moniker!

Historic inscription beside Utah 128   *4.A. Barnes*

In the early 1880s, a young man named Victor Hanson homesteaded a parcel of land near a recently-constructed narrow-gauge railroad in what is now known as the Cisco Desert. Hanson had the foresight to recognize the location as a potentially lucrative travel stopover. He built a restaurant, a hotel, and eventually some other amenities that would appeal to travelers. This was the birth of the town of Cisco. Later, sheep and cattle ranchers moved in to add to the growth of the little town. With the advent of automobile travel, U.S. 6, the main east-west artery, was constructed. Cisco thrived for about seventy years but, with the decline of the narrow-gauge railroad and, later, the construction of Interstate 70 bypassing it two miles to the north, it faded out and became a ghost town. A few crusty old characters still remained in the deserted buildings until a fire in the late 1970s demolished most of what was left of Cisco.

Ballard Harris lived in Cisco back in the 1940s and operated a little gas station there. The only electricity in Cisco, or even anywhere around Cisco, was provided by Ballard's big diesel-powered generator. Traffic along U.S. 6 wasn't exactly heavy back then, especially after dark, and Ballard probably closed up the station and hit the hay shortly after the sun went down.

Anyway, Ballard was well into sawing logs one night when his sub-conscious sort of registered the sound of that diesel engine starting up. Now, he was awake enough to know that he was the only one who ever started up that generator, and he was pretty darn sure he was still in bed. He sat up, yanked his boots on and headed outside to see who the heck was messing around with his generator. Then he heard an automobile pulling up to the gas pump. He was certain someone was up to no good, so he dashed back into the house and grabbed his trusty rifle. Well, that poor traveler who'd had the misfortune to need gas in the middle of the night got quite a start when Ballard came storming out of the house in his underwear and boots with his hair all awry, brandishing a shootin' iron like he meant to use it. Matter of fact, that flatlander got such a start that he laid shiny patches in the dirt where his rear tires spun out in his hurry to be gone!

In the early 1900s, the town of Moab had already been founded and plans were being laid for another town about 25 miles north of Moab and near the Denver-Rio Grande railroad, which was to be named Valley City. Howard Balsley, who lived in Seymour, Indiana, somehow got word of this development and decided he'd had enough of Seymour and wanted a piece of the action. Howard and his sister purchased a few chunks of land, sight unseen, in the proposed Valley City area. The developers built a dam, creating a reservoir for irrigation.

Howard Balsley and his sister purchased round trip tickets to Thompson's Spring, a tiny railroad town about seven miles east of the new Valley City. Howard's sister would return to Indiana shortly after surveying her investment, but Howard never made use of his return ticket. He stayed in the area for the rest of his life. When Howard arrived in Valley City, he was impressed with the potential of the settlement but still chose to make Moab his primary residence. It turned out to be a wise decision, because in a year or two, a "one-hundred-year flood" swept through Valley City, resulting in the near total destruction of the community.

Howard Balsley was a man of intelligence and courage. He didn't let the financial setback thwart his plans to remain in the area. He realized, however, that he needed some type of income, so he approached various people in order to feel out the job market in this remote desert town. Someone suggested that he check with the U.S. Forest Service, which he did. He was hired on the spot.

Being a ranger put Balsley in a position to meet a number of people engaged in prospecting for all kinds of ore. He became interested in mining, especially vanadium mining, and set out to become something of a prospector himself. In his early mining days, Balsley actually shipped ore to Madame Curie for her radium experiments.

While increasingly successful in his mining enterprise, Balsley also worked for the United States Bureau of Indian Affairs. During the early 1920s, there was a problem locally with bands of renegade Indians. Posey and Poke were the two ringleaders. Balsley had some close encounters with both of these characters. On one occasion, Chief Posey came upon him while Balsley was off his horse, believing he had Howard at a distinct disadvantage. Howard was standing by his horse, however, and, unbeknownst to Posey, had a pistol in his saddle boot which he could easily have reached had he deemed it necessary. Wisely, Howard recognized that he probably would never make it out of there alive if he shot Posey. So he was congenial and accommodating and pretty soon Posey realized that he wasn't going to scare this white man. That sort of took all the fun out of it for Posey, and he left peacably.

Another run-in with the Indians occurred when Howard and a government man from Washington were sitting around their campfire one evening. Howard sensed that there was someone nearby, watching them. When he looked behind him, there was a semicircle of Indians half surrounding them. The Washington man was terrified.

"Wh-what are we gonna do now, Mr. Balsley?" he asked.

"Invite 'em to dinner," Howard replied calmly.

So the two motioned for the Indians to come over to the fire and eat, which they did. After having eaten their fill, the Indians nodded to the men and left.

Howard always seemed to have a liking for Indians, despite the fact they frequently took advantage of him. In the early 1970s I saw old Howard out in his yard one afternoon and stopped to chat. During the conversation, I learned that he had loaned an Indian friend his 1958 Ford the previous week. He was still wondering when and if it would be returned!

Ross Musselman and his son Rusty were from New York. Ross spent a lot of his time working with YMCA groups in the city. In the late 1920s, his health began to deteriorate and he started thinking about moving to a drier, warmer climate. When he heard about Moab, Utah, he conceived the notion of developing a guest ranch specifically aimed at accommodating young, inner-city boys who never had the opportunity to experience anything but city life. Ross and Rusty moved out to Moab in 1929.

The Musselmans had an uncle who already lived in Moab. Roy Musselman was a trapper out of Walla Walla, Washington. A serious problem with wolves had developed in the Four Corners area and the creatures were destroying hundreds of cattle. The wolves would often kill far more than they could eat, frequently costing ranchers as much as 800 dollars a night, quite a sum in those days. The attacks seemed to have a pattern. Every eight to ten days, the pack would make a complete circle through New Mexico, Arizona, Utah and Colorado. Coyotes and foxes followed the wolves at a safe distance, picking over the carcasses of the dead animals. The local ranchers had called Roy and asked him to come down and see what he could do about the problem. Within a year after he accepted the challenge, he had trapped and killed thirteen of the fourteen wolves. A cowboy shot the fourteenth.

Anyway, Ross and Rusty set about fulfilling their dream. They bought a little ranch with some acreage on Pack Creek at the base of the La Sal Mountains. Soon the boys' ranch was operating; there was a large guest house, several smaller cabins, and a chuckhouse with a huge kitchen, barbecue pit, and recreation room. After a few years, the boys' ranch went coed and, later, became a dude ranch for paying tourists who wanted to play cowboy on their vacations. Ross and Rusty grazed cattle on the adjoining pasture in the summer and wintered their cattle in the bottoms, driving their herd through the canyons in the spring and fall to rotate pasture land.

Rusty eventually married a gal named Lily and they decided to move down onto the Navajo reservation. Rusty spoke a little Navajo and he and Lily decided to start a trading post. They bought the existing Cow Canyon

Trading Post, a little establishment which was not doing an exceptionally lucrative business and whose owners wanted out. Rusty traveled throughout the reservation, buying and trading wool and lambs with the Indians. Through his efforts, the business started picking up again. The Indians apparently liked Rusty, because when their Deputy Sheriff retired, they approached Rusty to replace him. He accepted. Shortly thereafter, the Sheriff fell ill and the Navajos again prevailed upon Rusty to fill the higher position. This promotion involved a move to Monticello, Utah, where Rusty and Lily remain to this day.

Jimmy Hewett and Henry Rose originally homesteaded what is now Rusty Musselman's place in Monticello. Jimmy and Henry were eating breakfast one morning when a couple of riders came tearing up on foaming, panting horses. Being friendly fellows, Jimmy and Henry invited the men to join them for breakfast. Being peaceable fellows, Jimmy and Henry asked the men to hang up their guns before sitting down to eat. The men complied courteously enough, but something about them just didn't set well with Henry. After breakfast, Jimmy walked outside with their guests to check on the horses. The two men were eager to be on their way and kept asking Jimmy if he'd be willing to trade horses with them. Meanwhile, Henry's mistrust got the better of him and, just to be on the safe side, he pilfered their firearms. When the two men came back inside the cabin, they were looking down the barrels of their own guns and being politely asked to leave. As it turned out, Henry's intuition was right on the button. The two men had robbed a bank upstate and had come through the Monticello area on their way south, probably to Mexico. They must have fallen into an argument shortly after Henry ran them off, because one of them was later found dead over in Boulder Canyon.

About forty years later, after Rusty and Lily bought the old homestead, Henry stopped by and asked permission to look for the guns he had taken from the bank robbers. He had buried them in a cave across the wash from the ranch house. Sure enough, he found the hidden guns, still in perfect condition.

One day, Jimmy decided it was high time to buy one of those newfangled but increasingly popular items - a Model T Ford. Now, back in those days, when someone bought a car, the dealer simply had it delivered to the buyer. This was the case with Jimmy's new car. Ordinarily, this would be a real convenience, not having to go to the city to pick up the new car. The one fly in the ointment, however, was the fact that the fellows had no idea how to drive. To make matters worse, they didn't know anyone who *did* know how to drive and could show them how to operate the fool thing. So they came in from riding their horses one day and there sat the car in the yard. There was a ten- or fifteen-foot drop-off not far behind the spot where the car had been parked. Jimmy immediately wanted to try it out, so he hopped in the driver's seat.

"Can you drive it?" asked Henry.

"Oh, sure! No problem," answered Jimmy.

So Jimmy promptly put the car in reverse and stomped on the gas pedal. The car shot backwards right over the edge of the embankment and landed on its rear bumper. There it stood, with its nose pointing straight up in the air. Jimmy got knocked around inside the car a bit and opened up a nasty gash on his head that was bleeding like crazy. Henry decided he'd better sew it up before Jimmy lost much more blood, as Jimmy was plenty lightheaded in his normal state. The boys were used to doing their own "mending," since they had always lived miles away from the nearest doctor, so this was no big deal. The only problem in this particular instance was that the last sewing Henry had done was putting buttons on his coat and some-how he'd left a button on the already-threaded needle. In his haste to put poor Jimmy's noggin back together, he ended up sewing that big coat button right smack dab in the middle of Jimmy's forehead. Jimmy didn't mind, however, in fact, he was right proud of that button and showed it off to everybody he saw!

Rusty and his hand, Garland Douglas, needed some good riding horses to be used on the dude ranch. They figured Jimmy and Henry knew horses like no one else, so they looked the boys up and found that they had gone into the chicken-raising business. They had literally thousands of chickens, but no horses. It was getting late, so Henry and Jimmy insisted Rusty and Garland stay at their place for the night. The next morning they were served eggs for breakfast, a rare treat for many folks in those parts. They ate eggs 'til they were blue in the face. Eggs piled six high. Rusty and

Garland ate so damn many eggs that morning it was nearly a year before they could bear to look at another egg!

Thirty-eight miles south of Moab and on the east side of Highway 191 is a huge, dome-shaped rock named Church Rock. I have asked a number of locals how it received that name because it doesn't really look like a church or cathedral at all. I have yet to receive a logical answer. A few maintain that it was so named because it is situated near where a church was established by Marie Ogden, a fervently religious woman with some very unusual notions.

Church Rock   *F.A. Barnes*

Rusty Musselman knew Marie Ogden and spoke highly of her and her many talents. She was an accomplished pianist and had taught piano in New York City. When she moved west, she couldn't part with her beautiful piano and had it shipped to her home in Photograph Gap, which is about five miles west of the turnoff to Canyonlands National Park. According to Rusty,

Mrs. Ogden was also president of The Women's Federation of America at one time. Apparently, her religious bent developed in the early days of the depression, although Rusty couldn't speculate as to the cause. Marie believed that Church Rock had some connection with the prophesy that Christ was going to return one day and that, upon his return, he would land right on top of that rock of hers. She kept this white donkey tied up at the base of the rock and Christ was supposed to hop on it when he got there and ride the donkey over to Marie's Garden of Eden, where water would miraculously spout out of the rocks.

Curiously enough, Mrs. Ogden managed to attract some wealthy followers to her fold. She got them to pool their money and turn it over to her, then she would allot them seven cents a day to live on. They were vegetarians and had well-kept gardens. They also had a herd of milk cows, and no one seemed undernourished or unhappy.

Remnants of the Home of Truth   *F.A. Barnes*

The Home of Truth, as it was called, existed for a number of years without problems, but nothing remains blissful forever. One of Marie's many teachings provided that none of the members of her sect would ever die; that Christ's return would occur during their lifetimes, thereby protracting the life span of the faithful indefinitely. Now, this presented a bit of a problem, especially when one of the faithful did eventually have the temerity to keel over dead. Marie was quick to respond that the expired woman's life would be restored and that this must be a sign of the coming of Christ. So they put the body in a safe place and kept an eye on it. In a week or so, Marie called the believers to her side to observe the movement of the body that signified its "return to life." Turns out it was actually maggots crawling around underneath the dead gal's clothes that created the illusion of movement. Well, between that little occurrence and the ruckus raised by the San Juan County Board of Health as a result, the sect began to disperse. I guess even the prospect of eternal life can kind of tend to lose its appeal under certain circumstances.

Home of Truth building, Photograph Gap   *F.A. Barnes*

Rusty Musselman was one of the first people ever to have familiarized himself with the area now known as the Needles District of Canyonlands National Park. He was driving four-wheeled vehicles around that area before there were even any roads, and he actually made some of the roads himself.

Not long after Canyonlands was awarded national park status, Rusty was traveling in the area and was stopped by a young ranger. The ranger was very courteous as he explained to Rusty that he was not permitted to travel on the road that he was on. Rusty replied, " *Well, I don't know why not! I built this road!*" This caught the young ranger off guard and he apologized and allowed Rusty to proceed.

Rusty once told me a story that he read in a journal when he was very young about a mining camp cook who froze to death. Latigo Gordon was the head honcho of the mining camp and he and the other miners decided that the cook should have a decent burial. The ground was frozen and they were only able to dig a shallow grave about two feet deep. There they laid the cook to rest and, since they were not insensitive to the needs of the dead, they put a gallon jug of whiskey in with him in case he should need it on his journey to the hereafter.

Then they went on to Monticello and held a wake. They partied and raised hell until the whiskey all ran out. Still powerful thirsty, not to mention bereaved at the loss of the only feller in the camp who could cook, they debated about going back to the grave and reclaiming the bottle of whiskey they'd put there. The cook, they decided, was a decent sort and wouldn't mind their borrowing his jug - they could always bring him back a new one later. So they headed back for the cook's grave. But when they got there and exhumed the body, the whiskey was all gone! Those boys were a mite shook up when they arrived back in camp - until they saw Latigo Gordon lounging by the fire, drunker'n a thousand Indians at a snake dance! He had beaten them to the draw!

Angel Arch in the winter - see Chapter 14

CHAPTER TWENTY-ONE

THE FLORIDA CONNECTION

One day, George West, Jr. from southwestern Florida called and said he'd heard that I knew the Moab area quite well and asked if I'd take him and his wife on a four-wheel-drive tour. I told him I could but that there was a hitch. There are several local companies who are licensed to conduct tours into the parks and also areas on the perimeter. I frequently drove for these companies and didn't wish to cut into their business. Therefore, I explained, if I did take George and his wife out on tour, I couldn't accept payment. George agreed to these conditions, but insisted that he would make it worth my while even if I wouldn't take any money.

We had a delightful day in the Klondike Bluffs area of Arches National Park. After leaving the park, I took them over into a region west of the airport. I don't recall exactly what happened but somehow we got stuck for a little while and had to utilize the low range of the four-by-four. It was the first time George had even been in a four-wheel-drive vehicle and he was impressed. Two years later, George and Norma came back for another junket and asked me to take them to the Island-in-the- Sky. We did the Shafer Trail and the "Neck" overlook and that's all it took. They were in love with the place! With Grand View Point and the Green River Overlook behind us, we began looking for a place to eat our lunch. When we did stop and spread out our vittles, a bold coyote came right up to the Scout and begged for food! We shared our lunch with him and George and Norma were delighted.

Whenever I took the Wests out, one of their stipulations was that I join them for dinner at a local restaurant that evening. During this series of tours, George kept insisting that I come to Florida and let him show me the Everglades. Little did I realize that, the following year, I would take him up on his offer.

When things are going like a song, we are inclined to take life for granted and forget to count our blessings. In March, 1986, my beloved wife Jean was diagnosed as having cancer. Determined as we both were that she would survive this dreaded disease, and despite her valiant struggles against it, Jean died on August 19, 1986. A part of me went with her. After 38 won-

Jean and Fred, 1948

derful years together, life without her was inconceivable.

I was miserable with Jean gone and decided to go to Florida to spend Christmas with my daughter, Elaine, in St. Petersburg. I had ridden my Indian Scout motorcycle to Florida back in 1941 along the Tamiami Trail, which runs from Miami to Naples, and decided to take the same route this time in my Toyota Celica.

It was good to be with my daughter and her family, but after a few days I got restless and decided to drive down to Cape Coral where George West, Jr. lived and see if he was around. I had only his phone number and post office box so I called him upon my arrival. He was excited to hear that I was in town and immediately began throwing things together for our trip to the Everglades, as he had promised the previous year. Within a few hours of my arrival, we hopped in his big Chevy Suburban and were off.

George took me to "Alligator Alley" and showed me alligators, swamps, royal hammock trees and even a swamp buggy. He showed me where the old railroad went through the jungle. He took me through the remote village of Copeland, then on south to the towns of Everglades and Chokoloskee. On our return along the old Tamiami Trail we passed a number of Seminole Indian camps. I enjoyed George's tour immensely and tried to commit as much as I could to memory, because I knew I'd be back.

About a year later, Harry Beach, my friend from Hartford, Connecticut, called me to take him on a tour of the Everglades. I was surprised that he wanted a desert rat like me to guide him through a Florida swamp! He'd been to Moab at least fifty times and I had shown him a different backcountry playground just about every time. I guess he thought that, since I was so knowledgeable when it came to acting as a guide in the desert, I'd have the same knack when it came to 'gator country!

He knew I was going to St. Petersburg to visit my daughter and her family, so he and his copilot, Glenice Fluiery, flew Harry's Mooney down and met me at the St. Petersburg airport. I had driven there in my Toyota Celica a few days in advance. This 2,500-mile trip had first taken me to visit friends in Indianapolis, then on to my daughter's home.

My biggest concern was finding the right road that would take us into the same area that George West, Jr. had shown me. I was going to try to duplicate his tour. My worries were unfounded, however, as I located the first proper turn right off the bat. I even located a hunter's shack that was so well hidden that access involved walking over a series of wooden planks suspended only inches above the water. There was a huge rope swing hanging from a tree, which I had tried out the previous year. We didn't see any snakes or alligators in this area, but did get scared silly when we were driving along a back road and a military fighter plane screamed by overhead at a very low altitude. We had no warning and the plane was probably doing over 500 mph! The roar of the jet engines was deafening and it was a wonder I didn't run right into the ditch, I was so startled! We did get to see a couple of alligators along Highway 41 later in the trip.

On my first trip with George West, he had told me about his cabin near the Kissimmee River, so the following year I again visited Florida and he urged me to spend a night and a day with him and Norma Lee at the cabin. They fed me dinner, then we sat around and planned the following day's activities. Later that evening, though, I got very sick to my stomach and was up most of the night. In the morning, I didn't feel much better, but I wanted to go for a ride in the swamp buggy, so I tried to tough it out. The swamp buggy was built on a 1929 Ford Model A frame. We made a big loop through the swamps but, as much as I enjoyed it, I seemed to get sicker by the minute. So we returned to the cabin and I reluctantly told George that I was going to have to head back to St. Petersburg. At first, I didn't think I would be able to make the whole trip in one leg, but by the time I reached Tampa, my stomach was feeling much better and I continued on to St. Petersburg.

Not long after my last trip to Florida, George's wife Norma Lee passed away. He needed to get his mind off his grief so he decided to come to Moab. I made arrangements to take him for a little ride up Onion Creek. Lin Ottinger, a longtime guide and explorer, was probably the first to conduct tours into Onion Creek and on up to Polar Mesa. It has always been one of Lin's favorites, and with good reason.

Along the Onion Creek trail   G.A. Barnes

In the early days of our Onion Creek jaunts, we would often have to "build" the road on our way in. The road crosses the creek in more than thirty places and, from time to time, minor washouts occur. More recently, however, the road has been in good shape and is actually passable with a two-wheel-drive vehicle most of the time.

The old 1970 Scout had been chugging along without any problem, but I began to hear a tinkling sound that worried me a bit. Apparently George didn't hear it, or chose to ignore it, because he said nothing. I thought, *"If I can just break out on top where the ranch is, I might be able to call it a day and turn around and go back!"*

Finally, the tinkling sound got to George, too, and we decided we'd better stop and see if we could pinpoint the trouble. After some examination, it became apparent that we had a small radiator problem, but I thought we could make it the remaining one mile to the flat area. Wrong! With a hideous noise, the fan went into the radiator and coolant and water sprayed everywhere!

We hadn't seen another soul the whole trip and weren't likely to. We got the tools out and took the upper shroud off the radiator. Next we got the fan belt and fan off. Using the creek bank, we managed to get the Scout turned around and pointing back the way we had come. We gathered up all our tools and parts and put them in the Scout and, fingers crossed, began rolling downhill. There was no water left in the radiator, so we didn't dare use the engine except to get over small rises. Boy, was it a long trip back to Utah 128! We made it, though, and the first vehicle we saw was driven by a girl I knew. I flagged her down and George rode into town with her. She dropped him off at a phone booth and he called my wife to come and get him. He then got his Suburban and came back to get me and the crippled Scout.

George still returns to Moab just about every year to go out into the backcountry with me. I'll swear, some people are just gluttons for punishment!

CHAPTER TWENTY-TWO

BINKS

Art and Binks Martin had been friends of Jean's and mine for many years. Art was a retired Forest Service man and an enthusiastic motorcycle rider and we had always enjoyed swapping two-wheeler tales. When Jean and I bought our ten acres in Kayenta Heights, Art helped build our house. The four of us sang in the Community Baptist Church choir.

We first met when Jean and I took our dunebuggy up the Sand Flats road for a little jaunt. Art and Binks were up there with some friends from out of town. We got to talking and our new friends expressed curiosity about the dunebuggy. Binks said she had never ridden in such a contraption, so I offered to take her for a quick spin. I strapped her in and took off toward the slickrock - a little faster than necessary, I must admit. When I left the road and headed up a slickrock dome, Binks' eyes got as big as saucers.

"What are you doing? You aren't going up there! No! No! Yes, you are! Let me outta this thing!"

Dunebuggy on Sand Flats slickrock   *J.A. Barnes*

Her pleas were in vain. In a couple of minutes we had reached the top of the 300-foot dome. By this time, I was feeling a bit ashamed of myself for having subjected Binks to something so foreign to her. I was a little concerned she might try to climb out and walk back down, so I quickly began the descent to the road. Years later, she admitted to me that she had begged Art to refuse if I ever offered them a jet boat tour!

On Christmas day in 1979, Art complained of severe chest pains. Binks rushed him to the hospital. Art died as he walked into the emergency room. Binks was a very brave lady and carried on like a trooper, and Jean and I saw a lot of her.

Seven years later, I lost Jean to cancer. It never even occurred to me that some day I might find someone to fill her shoes. I wasn't sure I even wanted to. But life is full of little surprises.

My friend Binks called me one day to see if I would take her and some friends out four-wheeling. I told her I'd be happy to. Binks packed a picnic lunch and we drove up Onion Creek. We stopped to enjoy our noon-time meal, then continued on to Polar Mesa. On our return, we took the La Sal Mountain Loop Road back to Moab. Binks was wearing a pretty blue sweater, so I suggested we stop and take some pictures. All too soon, the journey ended. Binks' guests had thoroughly enjoyed the trip and I had to admit that I had thoroughly enjoyed Binks!

Binks

I was captivated. I couldn't deny that being with Binks stirred up feelings I thought I'd never have again. One Sunday afternoon, we were walking in the sand down by the river and I startled myself by proposing marriage to her and she actually accepted! On January 14, 1989, Binks and I were joined in matrimony at the Moab Community Baptist Church.

My son Bernie now teaches school in Moab, and I'm very fond of his wife Paula. My daughter Elaine still lives in Florida with her husband Jim, who is on the police force, and her kids, Shane and Cody. Binks' son Jim lives in Anchorage, Alaska, with his wife Billie, and two children, Lori and Jason. Binks' daughter and her husband Ray live in Gunnison, Colorado, with their youngsters, Joel, Alex, and Grant.

I had never had any great desire to see Alaska until I married Binks. She had been up there fourteen or fifteen times. She and Art drove up with their Bronco and trailer one year, but Binks preferred flying. The more Binks talked Alaska to me, the better it sounded. My first trip up there was in 1990 and I loved it! Jim was an excellent guide. This had rubbed off on Binks and, between the two of them, they sold me on Alaska! Enough so that I was glad to learn that Binks' granddaughter was to be married in August of 1991. It would give me another excuse to go there!

As we had done the year before, we drove the car over to Grand Junction, Colorado and flew to Salt Lake City on a small Fairchild. We had a short layover before boarding the flight to Anchorage. We arrived about 2:00 a.m. and Jim and his family were at the airport to meet us. While Jim was bringing his van around to the baggage pickup area, Jim's wife and Binks lined up at the entrance to the luggage conveyor belt. The gals kept an eye peeled for the bags as they came out of the chute. They didn't have to wait very long before the first two came through. We quickly loaded these into the waiting van, then ran back for the third bag.

Jim and Billie had a houseful so Binks and I stayed at the nearby home of some friends, John and Vida Nelson. We were getting ready for bed and Binks went to get her little overnight bag and my shaving kit out of the canvas suitcase they were in. When she opened it, she found it full of sweatshirts and other items we'd never seen before! A quick look at the name tag revealed that it belonged to someone from California. So we knew that the first thing we'd have to do in the morning would be to call the airport and arrange to switch bags.

When I started to open the other suitcase, I found it was locked so I asked Binks where the keys were. She replied that she never locked that suitcase, as she'd lost the keys years before. So we went to bed with all this on our minds and, needless to say, neither of us did much sleeping. We were up at 6:00 a.m. and slipped quietly out of the house in order not to awaken our hosts. We walked over to Jim and Billie's to see if Jim had a hacksaw so we could get into the locked suitcase. He didn't, so we walked back to John and Vida's. We explained our predicament to Vida and she looked through John's tools and found a hacksaw. I got busy with it and soon had the lock sawed off. Upon opening it, we found *this* one also full of clothes Binks had never seen before!

So there we were, stuck with two bags identical to ours, no clothes to wear, and a bad case of morning breath from not having our toothbrushes! Binks called the airport and they said they had a couple of folks there from California who were in a similar pickle!

We borrowed the Nelsons' van and took the bags to the airport and made the swap. If nothing else, this taught us a valuable lesson. From then on, regardless of how tired we are, we check the name tags on the luggage before ever leaving the airport!

Delicate Arch

CHAPTER TWENTY-THREE

FRIENDS

After 72 years, I must say that I retain the indomitable spirit and zest for adventurous living that has made my life so much fun. One of my greatest pleasures has been making so many wonderful friends and keeping in touch with them. There's a lot of satisfaction in receiving letters and phone calls from dear friends all over the world. Unfortunately, some of those friends are no longer around, and one of the purposes of this chapter is to dedicate a little space to their memories. This may not be important to the reader, but it is to me, so I beg indulgence.

I'd like to remember Chuck Calkins, my dear friend who recently passed away after a courageous battle with cancer. Young J. D. Rogers, my companion on the hair-raising trip through snowy Kansas, is now gone and I miss him. Ed Hayes, a guy I greatly admired for his knowledge of southeastern Utah, lost his life when the rock outcropping on which he was standing, at the viewpoint overlooking the big bend in the Colorado River, crumbled and gave way. Ed fell more than 500 feet to his death. Ironically, almost all the guides and probably half of the tourists in canyon country have stood in that exact same place at one time or another.

I'm sure there are more friends I've loved and lost whose names should appear here but, alas, I cannot remember everyone. I hope I may be forgiven for anyone I have missed.

I also want to do a little name-dropping as well. There are and have been so many colorful characters in and around canyon country that I haven't had time or space to go into detail about them personally or into the history of their families, but they deserve mention.

Joe Folk is one of my old motorcycle buddies from Indiana who fell in love with Utah's canyon country. He spent some time running shuttle buses for Tex's Tours and later bought a few acres of property in Kayenta Heights near our place. He helped me with the construction of our house and I just wanted to thank him for being such a good friend for so many years.

Art Green, who ran airboat tours up the Colorado, and Harry Goulding, who established Goulding's Trading Post in Monument Valley, were cousins. Both boys were apparently born with an adventurous and mischievous spirit and were known to have actually held up the Durango-Silverton narrow-gauge train when they were thirteen years old! Naturally, they were caught. Their grandmother succeeded in getting them out of the scrape and they both grew up to be respectable businessmen.

Harry Goulding's daughter married Norman Nevils, a river guide who was also a buddy of Barry Goldwater's. Norm died in a plane crash over Mexican Hat, Utah.

Art Chaffin was a rancher who maintained the primitive road from Hanksville to the Hite Ferry. Art and another cowboy discovered the area that is now Goblin Valley State Park.

The Ekker family has been ranching in southern Utah about as long as anyone can remember. Butch Cassidy and his bunch often holed up at Art Ekker's place. Art's son, A. C. Ekker, still runs the ranch.

Another colorful family in the area are the Hunts. They've been here about as long as the Ekkers and are spread all over the place. Just about everybody who grew up in southeastern Utah has a Hunt for a relative!

Pearl Bittlecomb Baker, daughter of Joe Bittlecomb, another old desert coot, was a well-known writer. Pearl's son, Joe Baker, used to run the Green River in a large boat powered by three outboard motors. Joe is, sadly, no longer with us, and Pearl passed away at age 85 in December, 1992.

Bert Loper was another pioneer river rat from Green River. Bert took many raft trips into the hitherto unknown regions below the confluence of the Green and Colorado rivers. He met his death on one such trip.

The Taylors are one of the oldest ranching families in the Moab area and have run cattle on the La Sal Mountains for decades.

On a final note, I thank my family, friends and acquaintances for giving me the inspiration to write this book. As it is largely a collection of anecdotes and memories, I'm sure I will, from time to time, remember humorous little occurrences and poignant moments that I will wish I had included. Perhaps these will provide the material for another book! I also thank my readers for giving me the opportunity to share my experiences. I hope they have furnished some humor and enjoyment.

MOAB, UTAH, 1993

The Moab economy has fluctuated throughout the years. Based primarily on vanadium and copper mining in the 1930s and '40s, it really took a hike when, in the 1950s, Charlie Steen discovered that the area was also rich in uranium, an ore which wasn't exactly in great demand until the end of World War II. There was a lot of oil and gas drilling activity around the area until the early 1980s, when the slump in the mineral industry took its toll.

Also affected by this lull were the local mining operations. Because the uranium mines had stockpiled large quantities of ore, operations at some of the mines were completely shut down; others were cut back drastically. Hundreds of families either sold their homes or let them be foreclosed upon, and moved from the area. There was always a fairly dependable seasonal tourist trade, but not enough to sustain the town through the winter.

Moab fell into an economic depression for a few years during the 1980s, until the recently-popular sport of mountain biking helped revive the little community. Droves of enthusiastic young people began pouring into town in their quest for thrills on the slickrock hills. This novel sport and its proponents injected new blood into the suffering little burg. Existing businesses were given facelifts, new enterprises were established, motels and supermarkets sprang up overnight.

Now, in the 1990s, a rejuvenated Moab boasts a healthy economy based in tourism.

Moab, aerial photograph   F.A. Barnes